PERFORMANCE
& PURPOSE
IN DYING & DEATH

C K HOGAN

First published in 2022 by
Free Association Books

A CIP Catalogue of this book is available from
the British Library

ISBN: 978-1-91138-373-4

Typeset by
Typo•glyphix
www.typoglyphix.co.uk

Cover design by
Chandler Book Design

Printed and bound in England

CONTENTS

Contents

Contents

Contents

FOREWORD

As a perspective of the dying process and the nature of death itself, it is the intention that this book might help us to accept and embrace both as a part of life, and that a shift in perception could alleviate some of the fear, resistance and denial surrounding death. Much has been written about this by spiritual teachers, psychologists, philosophers, and palliative specialists. This book is an entry into the conversation from a viewpoint that is not medical, religious, nor postulating any form of belief system. It is partly a survey of our attitude and resistance to dying and death, and an examination of the options available that could serve as a non-denominational enquiry into an unavoidable eventuality. The principal tenet is that the tools required for this shift in perception and understanding that would allow us to drop the heavy weight of fear and anxiety are to be found within us – we already possess them. It's a case of knowing where to look and recognising the most direct route for each of us. There is no need to believe anything or anyone; peace lies in the knowing which arises from the validity of our own experience.

From a scientific materialist perspective these ideas may lack the sort of measurable evidence that is usually required. It is suggested that the science of mind and consciousness is the path for scientists and philosophers alike, and is how the single reality that is the source of all experience is to be made apparent. Some eminent scientists, physicists, biologists, and cosmologists are very far along the philosophical path (Bernardo Kastrup, Rupert Sheldrake, Richard Tarnas), and their perception, understanding and sense of purpose in the dying process, and the subsequent experience of consciousness after the body expires, embraces the spirituality of scientific enquiry, and seeks far beyond the confines of the materialist world view.

Art can act as a type of bardo between levels of consciousness but, as Picasso famously said, all art lies, and that includes words. The truth is ineffable, but while we are here, in this form, we still attempt to understand and explain it. We also try to come to terms with the inevitability of death by searching for clues and signs that point out what it might be beyond the physical fact of it. The possible continuation of conscious experience causes intense anxiety for many, even those who believe that there won't be any, which is probably more in hope than belief. As Xavier Comella said to his friend in *When I Was Mortal – Everything Bad Comes Back* by Javier Marias,

> *"I'm convinced that consciousness is the source of man's greatest suffering and there's no cure for it, no way to blunt it, the only end is death, though even that you can't be sure of."*

It is hoped that some of the signposts in this book will point the way to reducing the tension and suffering surrounding the mystery of death. These will include discussing the paradoxical nature of the divine and the mortal, of science and spirituality and the fear of relief. They will also address the subjects of grief, loss, and attachment with a view to understanding what we believe will be lost both when we die, or when someone close to us dies. Although Buddhism is most often used as an example of spiritual activity, there is no implication that this is the only prism through which we should contemplate issues surrounding dying and death. Because Buddhism is more philosophy than religion and because it doesn't involve worshipping any concept of god, it can offer a clearer perspective into the realms of spirituality unencumbered by belief systems that can, understandably, cause resistance. In fact, a precept throughout the book is that no belief system is ever required, that an enquiry into personal experience is always more valid. If there is an overall philosophical viewpoint, it is that of perennialism, thereby embracing the truth underlying all spiritual practices and philosophies. (Philosophia Perennis is referred to specifically in chapter 5.)

The consideration of the paradoxes and contradictions in our attitude to and perception of the end of life, the importance that we place on meaning and value together with a much broader and expansive understanding of transformation and conscious awareness, form the performance and purpose of this text on dying and death.

CHAPTER 1

DENIAL

The denial of death creates a sense of immortality, but a sense of it that we are neither prepared to confront nor defend. The truth is that we are immortal, and that death is illusory; deliberate and conscious denial of death is the understanding of what dies and what does not. The opposite of death is not life, which has no opposite; it just is, and this is-ness is unassailable and constant. Birth is the other side of death and birth is cyclic and regenerative. Birth and death occur in a multitude of guises in our daily lives. The pattern of waking, activity and sleeping is universal, not only in human beings, but in the cosmos, in the macrocosm and the microcosm. Death is frequently referred to as sleep in the language we often use to soften its impact and to make it more acceptable – pets are put to sleep rather than killed, and the phrase 'rest in peace' can be viewed as absurd if a belief in the end of consciousness is held. Sexual intercourse is another example of 'arising, abiding and cessation' and is referred to as 'le petit mort.' Little deaths happen on many levels everywhere, and to notice the rise and fall of existence in as many forms as we are capable of grasping is to heighten our awareness of the transitory nature of death and of the potentially joyful role that it could play in life.

Consciousness

> *"You cannot lose consciousness because it is, in essence, who you are. You can only lose something that you have, but you cannot lose something that you are... When forms around you die or death approaches, your sense of Beingness, of I Am, is freed from its entanglement with form: Spirit is released from its imprisonment in matter."*[1]

In *The Alchemy of Performance Anxiety,*[2] I explored the idea that if the act of performance was viewed from an altered perspective arising from the insights and suggestions developed in the book, then the experience of a focused, authentic, and communicative performance would be enhanced at many levels and could certainly be free from debilitating anxiety:

> *"One of the principal causes of fearing death is the unknown. But a stronger cause is the fear of complete isolation. Now, you wouldn't know you were in complete isolation unless you were conscious of being so, and many people believe*

---

1   Eckhart Tolle – A New Earth, Penguin Books, 2005

2   Free Association Books, 2018

that consciousness ends with the physical body. For those people, fear of death is non-sensical, yet they still have it. Furthermore, what is so dreadful about being alone? I suggest that the fear of isolation and all the associated 'causes' (rejection, judgement, criticism, failure) stem from lack of consciousness – deliberate, self-aware, internal consciousness. The experience of suddenly being you, all on your own with the expectation of accomplished artistic endeavour, can be overwhelming if you don't know who you are."

What, then, is consciousness? It is that which knows the experience of being; it is aware of itself and from this awareness imagination arises, and what we call 'matter'. As argued by Michael Bradford in *Consciousness: The New Paradigm (The Institute for Consciousness Research, 2017),*[3] it has an independent existence of its own and can enable the existence of physical form and therefore must be regarded as more 'real' than matter. As far back as 1890, William James said 'If evolution is to work smoothly, consciousness in some shape must have been present

---

3   The Institute for Consciousness Research, 2017

at the very origin of things. Accordingly, we find that the more clear-sighted evolutionary philosophers are beginning to posit it there.' One hundred and twenty-five years later:

"To begin with, we need to define more precisely what we mean by the word 'consciousness'. Although everybody has an intuitive understanding of it, the word itself is often overloaded with metaphysical assumptions. A materialist might define 'consciousness' as certain types of brain activity, while a religious person might define it as the essential attribute of an immaterial soul. In both cases, the word is overloaded with a particular explanation... I use the following definition in this book: consciousness is that whose excitations are subjective experiences. In other words, every subjective experience is a particular excitation of consciousness – whatever consciousness may intrinsically be – just like ripples are excitations of water. This operational definition is precise and metaphysically neutral." [4]

---

4   Bernardo Kastrup – Brief Peeks Beyond, 2015

This will be explored further in chapter 5 with the so-called hard problem of consciousness (as defined by David Chalmers in *The Conscious Mind 1996)* and the philosophy of panpsychism.

> Consciousness is that which knows the experience of being; it is aware of itself and from this awareness imagination arises, and what we call 'matter.' It is pure subjectivity.

Fear of Death

The fear of death is an egoic construct, the annihilation of which terrifies us throughout life. Any threat to it is always a source of anxiety and often of embarrassment. Death can be embarrassing both physically and psychologically because we are so accustomed to clinging to the illusion of permanence, control and even invincibility. Even though we may mouth words such as 'inevitability' and 'when my time comes', deep down it is as if it simply doesn't apply to us. Just as I suggested in *The Alchemy of Performance Anxiety*, to improve and transform our experience of artistic performance it is necessary to examine our day-to-day life performance which comprises thoughts, reactions, perceptions and interactions. In so doing, we can become aware of habitual behaviours that might be detrimental to any type of performance. This can be an ongoing exercise in observational awareness which then becomes a benign and beneficial habit.

With an understanding and acceptance of the nature of consciousness, the fear of death ought to fade and disappear. Even without that awareness, the fear of death is, rationally, absurd regardless of one's beliefs. Consider the amount of discomfort, physical self-criticism, dietary imposition and deprivation that so many people undergo through life, at war with their bodies and wishing that they occupied a different form. It should be a relief to be free from so much conflict which has taken up headspace and emotional energy over the years, even if it has only been a preoccupation with how to clothe it; we often use clothes as screens, distractions, and projections in our daily performances. It must be that we think and believe that our bodies (clothed or otherwise) are who we are, maintaining and reinforcing our sense of separateness. Bodies can be viewed as a cross between houses and cars; they need to be cared for in order to fulfil their function, a part of which is to shelter consciousness and enable it to travel when required.

However, even the most rational among us are still capable of fearing the process of dying and death, because fear is fundamentally irrational to begin with.

Flippant though that might sound, the fact is that we possess bodies that function like animals, yet our minds, capable of great feats of creation, have created an illusion of supremacy, and this duality is a source of conflict. 'Falling in love' ticks both boxes; our physicality is validated and made acceptable by a seemingly higher realm of existence, something pure and true. This mutual fascination has as much to do with our own relief as it does with the adoration of another. The guilt of being an animal is further alleviated when we reproduce – a double paradox perhaps. The cyclic nature of birth and death is perpetuated by sex, and alongside 'le petit mort' lies 'le grand mort' which is frequently denied by engaging in more of the activity. The issue of gender has now become much more fluid and, while it is increasingly accepted that one can feel housed in the wrong body and seek radical surgery to rectify it, there is a quest beyond gender realignment which is to transcend gender itself. Ernest Becker writes in *The Denial of Death:*[5]

---

5   The Denial of Death – The Free Press, 1973

"Man is aghast at the arbitrary nature of genitality, the accidentality of his separate sexual emergence. He can't accept the impermanence of the body casing or its incompleteness – now male, now female. The body makes no sense to us in its physical thingness, which ties us to a particular kind of fate, a one-sided sexual role. The hermaphrodite image represents a striving for wholeness, a striving that is not sexual but ontological. It is a desire of being for the recapture of the (Agape) unity with the rest of nature, as well as for a completeness in oneself. It is a desire for the healing of the ruptures of existence, the dualism of self and body, self and other, self and the world" [6]

Becker went on to write:

"Jung saw the wishful meaning and centrality of the hermaphroditic image with great clarity and historical sweep... Nothing is more eloquent and to the point than the words of a psychoanalytic patient... who 'condemned the abhorrent envelope of her body' by saying: "I

---

[6] See Appendix 1

wish I could tear this skin off. If I didn't have this stupid body, I would be as pure outside as I feel inside."'

There comes a time in the lives of many children when they are in disbelief that the Queen visits the lavatory – and even that their parents do (while the parents are still gods). Coming to terms with what Becker calls our 'creatureliness' can be a lifelong issue for many, and mechanisms of escape from it are evident everywhere in the form of distractions. Even menial, miserable, labour-intensive work can be preferable to asking the question. The experience of physical sensation is another reason for the body's existence – we are supposed to be experiencing and enjoying the world through our five senses and communicate it with others who are doing the same. The attitude of omnipotent deserving of a 'holiday' is another example of a paradoxical outlook. Holiday; holy day; hollow day. Anaesthetise the brain, assault the digestion, and burn the skin. Many who are likely to be afraid of death often do most to hasten it.

"The knowledge of death is reflective and conceptual, and animals are spared it... But to live a whole lifetime with the fate of death

haunting one's dreams and even the most sun-filled days – that's something else... Who wants to face up fully to the creatures we are, clawing and gasping for breath in a universe beyond our ken?" and:

"... everything that man does... is an attempt to deny and overcome his grotesque fate. He literally drives himself into a blind obliviousness with his social games, psychological tricks, personal preoccupations so far removed from the reality of his situation that they are forms of madness – agreed madness, shared madness, disguised and dignified madness, but madness all the same." [7]

Dying as Part of Life

We desire the same things in life as in death: freedom, peace, security, joy, and *the cessation of desire.* This might be difficult to imagine, but with the realisation that things, objects, and people don't ultimately satisfy us comes the insight that a sense of fulfilment must arise from within, that we possessed it all along. If we

[7] Ibid.

knew that we would experience these qualities as and when we die, we could anticipate it as the next stage in a cyclic journey rather than the end of a linear one. One way to experience this is to prepare, something that woefully few of us do. To prepare for death involves the same shift in attitude and perception as described above regarding performance. Death is a type of performance, and the necessary practice is intimately bound up with the practice of living.

For those who are highly sceptical of any form of post-physical consciousness, to ponder 'Pascal's Wager' might be useful. Blaise Pascal was a French thinker and mathematician well known for his work in probability theory. He stated that intelligence is unable to answer the question of life after death. If we make the intellectual gamble that there is and it transpires that there isn't, nothing is lost. However, if we assume otherwise, we might be completely adrift in an afterlife for which we have made no provision. On another occasion he also reflected 'Men are so necessarily mad that not to be mad would amount to another form of madness.'

The threat of loss is a significant feature of dreading death – the loss of people obviously, but also of property and experience.

Having said that preparing for death could be an integral aspect of life, indeed a way of life, let us consider the practicalities of this idea: what does it involve and what might we actually do? From a Buddhist perspective there is always plenty to do, and a practising Buddhist is constantly preparing for death by default through cultivating awareness and insight into the nature of impermanence and the true concept of wealth. The threat of loss is a significant feature of dreading death – the loss of people obviously, but also of property and experience. The Dalai Lama:

> "If one cultivates spiritual qualities such as mental harmony, humility, nonattachment, patience, love, compassion, wisdom and so forth, then one becomes equipped with a strength and intelligence able to deal effectively with the problems of this life; and because the wealth one is amassing is mental rather than material, it will not have to be left behind at

*death. There is no need to enter the after-death
state empty handed"* [8]

It was encountering death and human suffering that
caused *Siddhartha* Gautama (Shakyamuni Buddha) to
renounce his life of luxury and embark on a spiritual
search to discover the fundamental cause of and
solution to suffering 2,500 years ago. He wanted to
seek the *true cause* of the four life-states inherent and
inescapable in being human – birth, sickness, old age,
and death. The philosophy of Buddhism is frequently
among the most effective preparations for death by
non-Buddhists. Many writers and thinkers expound
what is fundamental Buddhist philosophy without
necessarily being aware of it. One such person was
Neville Goddard who wrote and lectured extensively
on transformation from within being the only path
to personal freedom. The recognition that we each
cause our experience through the mental states that
we choose to occupy is to be free from the debilitating
delusion that we are victims of circumstance. He
describes thought as the 'coin of heaven' and money
as its earthly equivalent. By this he means that our
thoughts determine our inner conversations which in

8   The Art of Happiness – Hodder & Staunton, 1998

turn manifest our experience. We should therefore be sure to think in terms of investment rather than 'drift on the tide of idle moods' whereby we squander the very source of our capital.

> *"It is only what is done now that counts. The present moment does not recede into the past. It advances into the future to confront us, spent or invested... Before us go the results of all that seemingly is behind. Not gone is the last moment – but oncoming"* [9]

He is really describing the transformative power of karma, of turning karma into purpose by undergoing what in Buddhism is known as human transformation or revolution. Through this we can change the very meaning of our past and do not have to carry a burden which apparently seals our fate, leaving us essentially powerless to act or determine our experience. Through our actions, we can create value and open the way to a new life starting from the present moment.

---

[9] Neville Goddard – Awakened Imagination, Merchant Books, 2015 edition

Death can feel to be something over which we have little or no control, and this makes us fearful. Preparation usually requires some form of application, and, although it might seem absurd to suggest that one can apply oneself to the dying process, that is what I'm doing here. In an interview with the writer and philosopher Eckhart Tolle, he was asked about his own attitude towards death and dying, to which he replied, 'Oh, I think I have already died.' William Blake also refers to the many deaths we experience during our lives. He said to his friend Crabbe Robinson:

"There is nothing like death. Death is the best thing that can happen in life; but most people die so late and take such an unmerciful time in dying. God knows, their neighbours never see them rise from the dead."

And in the year before his physical death:

"William Blake – one who is very much delighted with being in good company. Born 28th November 1757 in London and has died several times since."

In his *Books of the Dead*, Stanislav Grof writes about the possibility of experiencing near-death states without having to be in a life-threatening situation. These can be achieved through various forms of inner exploration which might include intense spiritual practice, psychedelic experience, certain forms of psychotherapy, and specific Shamanic and other transpersonal rituals.

> *"The experiential practice of dying, or "dying before dying" has two important consequences. It liberates the individual from the fear and changes his or her attitude towards dying, and so prepares him or her for the experiences at the time of biological demise, and by eliminating the fear of death, it transforms the individual's way of being in the world. For this reason, there is no fundamental difference between the preparation for death by exploration of dying, on the one hand, and spiritual practice leading to enlightenment, on the other. This is the reason why the ancient books of the dead could be used in both situations."* [10]

10 Stanislav Grof – The art of living and dying as told in the ancient BOOKS OF THE DEAD from Egypt, Tibet, the Americas and beyond. Thames & Hudson, 2013 edition

It is our awareness of these shifting altered states that could enable us to have control over the ones we choose to occupy. This is the practice, the preparation, and the performance. One might imagine that the denial of death must surely evaporate on receipt of a terminal diagnosis with a predicted time frame. The unavoidable truth must force us to confront the stark reality, and so come to terms with it far sooner than had been anticipated. Our entire perception must shift, and the stretched-out future of potential and possibility fall into the abyss. Where the main concerns might have been about varying aspects of domestic and financial life, suddenly none of it matters – nothing matters, because very soon there is to be nothing.

There are many and varied reactions to a terminal diagnosis, and although it may seem unavoidable, denial can still be one of them, and can adopt various guises. The physiology of shock exists to protect us, and often results in a delayed response to the fact that someone close has died, or that we are soon going to. Denial often takes this form - an emotional rejection of facts – which can function as a form of protection and as a coping mechanism. The feeling of disbelief is capable of lodging itself into the very core of our rejection, or non-acceptance, so that there's an almost solipsistic conviction that everyone else must be mistaken. The strength of denial can increase with the imminence of the event, and by absorbing oneself in tales of survival against atrocious odds, the power of the mind and/or spirit to overcome physical deterioration, and the faith of others to cast physical demons from a reluctant host, we are able to support and fortify the denial that has always been there, but which is suddenly required with unconscionable speed. What is the alternative to denial? Is it courage, and if so, what is that? Perhaps we think that courage is facing our fears and responding appropriately to whatever they seem to be. But the alternative to facing our fears can only be more fear, and so there is potential suffering either way. How courageous were soldiers at war when the penalty for desertion was execution? Or a suicide bomber when the fear of dishonour results in the infliction of suffering and death on innocent people. Fear of death takes many forms, and the courage to meet and even embrace it surely arises from living courageously, which means to be open to the risk of pain and loss and accepting our vulnerability to suffering. Parenting is one perfect example – it is a life-sentence from the very beginning. Courage surely arises from the recognition that we are more than an individual person, and it can enable us to transcend the limits of personal survival, whether we are in a warzone or in palliative care.

Letting Go

Near Death Experiences have been well documented and reflected on in Peter Fenwick's book *The Art of Dying* (Bloomsbury 2008), to which I will refer again later in chapter 5, where NDE will be discussed in more detail. The evidence arising from reports on them exactly describes the transformation aspired to without having to undergo such an experience. These include feelings of compassion, greater altruism, less egotistical preoccupation with fame and wealth and a deeper awareness of the nature of impermanence. Lama Zopa Rinpoche has described the concept of impermanence as the most important and beneficial thing that Shakyamuni Buddha could bequeath... the truth and reality of it. This is significant because a lack of understanding and acceptance around the idea of impermanence is the cause of so much suffering. It also provides a clear example of practice that we can habitually undertake in order to prepare for one of the great difficulties of the dying process – letting go. Letting go of the world, people, pets, property, possessions, experience. Also letting go of who we think we are and possibly awakening to the fact that we've been wrong for decades. *A Course in Miracles* provides 365 lessons in learning what is real and what isn't and sums itself up with this: *"Nothing real can be threatened. Nothing unreal exists."* [11]

Resistance to letting the body go hurts; in fact, apparently, it can be agony. Elisabeth Kubler-Ross studied and wrote about the five stages of dying and identified those who were unable to reach the fifth stage of acceptance as experiencing difficult and psychologically painful deaths, mainly because of their anger and the need to cling to what they imagined they were losing. Some believe that these are what ghosts are – people who have been unable to let go. In Buddhism, alaya-consciousness describes a store of karmic effects which can be transformed with the understanding and application of its philosophy. This is known as changing poison into medicine which, as I said above, is to create purpose and value out of negative past experience. If we know that we can control the quality of the transition, it stands to reason that we should make certain we are ready.

---

11 Foundation for Inner Peace – Penguin Books, 1975

Desire vs. Attachment

Developing the capacity to let go of earthly phenomena inevitably requires an understanding of the nature of desire and the difference between desire and attachment. It is often erroneously thought that Buddhists must overcome and somehow transcend desire because it arises from greed and selfishness, thereby causing suffering. The paradox of desire is that it can be both misguided and destructive while also being the 'driving force behind civilisation'.[12] The means of identifying the difference lies in the probable or actual outcome. Everyone experiences desires which cause behaviour that we know will be of no benefit to anyone and which we will almost certainly regret; these are deluded impulses. The cause of suffering is not desire in and of itself; it is the anger, greed and ignorance that motivated the deluded impulse. However, even the negativity of deluded impulses can be transformed into realisation through understanding and accepting the reality of birth and death. Daisaku Ikeda describes the transformation of the three paths into the three virtues. The three paths are earthly desires, karma,

---

12 P. Allwright – Basics of Buddhism, Taplow Press, 1999

and suffering, and the three virtues are truth, wisdom, and emancipation:

"In Nichiren's teaching of the three virtues... desires based on truth rather than delusion give rise to wise actions (good karma), which reduce the negative effects of our karma and free us of suffering... As a result, desires lead to enlightenment, not suffering." [13]

He goes on to confirm that it is the elimination of delusion rather than of desire that is necessary, and that through this even the sufferings associated with the death process can be transformed.

Throughout his writings Neville Goddard emphasised repeatedly the necessity for a strong desire as the powerful motivational force for manifestation. Desire and a controlled imagination are the creators and this, he says, is the truth that sets us free:

"The Truth that sets you free is that you can experience in imagination what you desire to

---

13 Daisaku Ikeda – Unlocking the Mysteries of Birth and Death, SGI, 2021

experience in reality, and by maintaining this experience in imagination, your desire will become a reality." [14]

Desire is essentially creative; attachment, however, is not. Desire is natural and can operate positively or negatively. Attaching our identities to the things we think we want causes suffering.

When we chant Namu Myoho Renge Kyo, rather than deny desire, we are encouraged to chant for what we most want and that is because desire is such a powerful driving force. We can ask for anything; the world and our senses exist to experience each other – we have only to ask, assume, accept, and receive. Desire is essentially creative; attachment, however, is not. When we become identified with the things (we think) we want, an attachment is formed, and this is where the suffering arises. Desire is a form of energy experienced through feeling, and can operate positively or negatively, in that we might want the

14 Neville Goddard – The Power of Awareness, Merchant Books, 2015 edition

cessation or absence of something as well as the manifestation of something. The fact remains that we wish things to be other than they are, right now in this present moment. Therefore, desire or wanting is natural and, as merely a preference that arises, it is neutral. We need not be defined or constrained by it – it happens, or it doesn't, no matter. The 'wanting mind' often develops a state of contingent living which is poor, because the present so often gets overlooked, and yet it was once wished for. Goals can be useful in helping us to focus intention as well as to promote growth and development, but not when they become a habitual distraction from the conscious awareness of the present moment which was either deliberately asked for or attracted by default.

Attachment arising from clinging to anything causes suffering in life, and so clinging onto life itself inevitably causes suffering in the dying process. The practice in life, therefore, is non-attachment. Acceptance of 'what is' in life is the most effective preparation for letting go in death.

At the close of Burnt Norton, the first of T.S. Eliot's Four Quartets, he writes:

"Desire itself is movement, /Not in itself desirable; /Love is itself unmoving, /Only the cause and end of movement, /Timeless, and undesiring /Except in the aspect of time / Caught in the form of limitation /Between un-being and being." [15]

End of Life Engagement

When people are dying, they tend to consider some, if not all, of the following at varying levels of engagement depending on their proclivities thus far: prayer, faith, forgiveness, and the possibility of God. The vocabulary will vary, but fundamentally these are the areas of preoccupation, quite possibly for the first time in some cases. The overriding tenet in this chapter is the suggestion that developing an awareness and understanding of these potential issues as we go through life is among the best form of preparation for the dying process, as and when it arrives – irrespective of one's personal viewpoints and beliefs. Without this process we are likely to revert to whatever the deep-seated underlying fear produces when we are confronted with the reality of death. Towards the end

---

[15] Faber & Faber paper covered Editions

of Evelyn Waugh's novel *Brideshead Revisited* there is the scene of capitulation when Lord Marchmaine, a life-long non-believer, succumbs to his fear and doubt on his deathbed and makes the Roman Catholic 'sign of the cross', to the dismay of some and delight of other members of his conflicted family. He was in no way prepared for death and so fear and doubt over-ruled a lifetime of apparently rational thought. There are a great many Jewish people who don't engage in religious practice at any level throughout the year with the exception of Yom Kippur which is the Day of Atonement, just in case it's all true, and so for twenty-four hours a year they adopt a spiritual insurance policy to cover all eventualities. It runs along similar lines to Pascal's Wager.

Prayer

Let's consider each subject in turn and attempt to define what they are and how they are perceived to operate. We will begin with prayer. It is generally accepted that to pray is to ask for something, whether it be mercy, forgiveness, wealth, freedom, security, a person, or an object. The key word is *for.* If we pray for anything it is because we don't already have it, in which case it has to happen in the future, if at all.

To whom are we praying? Who has the power to make these decisions about our experiences and life conditions? Who is the granter of wishes? When a Buddhist confronts the Gohonzon,[16] which is an object of devotion in the form of a scroll or *mandala* upon which the inscription *Namu Myoho Renge Kyo* appears down the centre, he sees a reflection of himself, of his life state as it is and, also, *as he wants it to be.* This Self is a conscious interaction between the super and sub-conscious minds and is wholly in the present tense. It is the Law of Assumption (discussed further in chapter 3) which operates through the feeling state of already being and possessing that which is desired. When we chant (*Namu Myoho Renge Kyo*) we yield to the feeling of fulfilment and know that *we* are the granter of wishes. We are looking at and praying to ourselves; we are acknowledging and experiencing our true nature.

---

16 The Gohonzon was inscribed by Nicherin (Dai) Shonin in mid 13th century Japan. Nam Myoho Renge Kyo contains the essence of the Buddhist teaching in the Lotus Sutra: namely, that everyone has the potential for Buddhahood and that life is eternal.

'Praying... is recognising yourself to be that which you now desire, rather than its accepted form of petitioning a God that does not exist for that which you now desire.[17]

Prayer is the art of preparing the site (your conscious awareness) to accept and receive the fulfilled wish by assuming its existence and being glad and grateful about it. It is the very opposite of effort. It is closer to meditation, a state that can be achieved when chanting and praying in the full consciousness that 'I am that'. Mary Oliver's poem 'Praying' –

"It doesn't have to be the blue iris, it could be weeds in a vacant lot, or a few small stones; just pay attention, then patch a few words together and don't try to make them elaborate, this isn't a contest but the doorway into thanks, and the silence in which another voice may speak."

---

17 Neville Goddard – At Your Command, Merchant Books, 2015 edition

Faith

Faith cannot easily be separated from prayer. Prayer has been defined here as the assumption of fulfilled desire, and so too is faith the assumption that the prayer will be realised.

> *"A miracle is the name given, by those who have no faith, to the works of faith. Faith is the substance of things hoped for, the evidence of things not seen."*

> Hebrews 11:1

Faith is both cause and attitude; it assumes, and it *knows*. Prayer brings a desired condition into consciousness and faith knows that it will manifest or indeed has done so already. To pray without faith is not only futile but completely absurd. Neither are the jurisdiction of any external agency, but both are solely dependent on one's own level of consciousness. What, then, is the difference between faith and belief? Faith doesn't need belief but, unless the power of the imagination is harnessed deliberately as an attitude, perception, and way of life, they might both contain an element, however small, of hope and, therefore, of doubt. No law has any room or scope for doubt because it would cease to be a law.

Transformation starts from within, and faith (knowing) is the cause; the manifested life state is the effect. This is alchemy, Buddhism, and lies within the perennial philosophy.[18]

> Prayer is the assumption of fulfilled desire, and faith is the assumption that the prayer will be realised.

Forgiveness and the Possibility of God

The true meaning of forgiveness needs some deep consideration and is often mistaken for a thought process and a decision, whereas it needs to involve feeling if it is to signify anything meaningful. To be meaningful it must be experienced, which is true of any transformation. FOR GIVE NESS means to use the power of the imagination (the ultimate creator) to move ahead and give (oneself and others) the revised version of events as they would like them to

18 See Appendix 3

have been. It is to see others as they would like to be seen and considered; to *assume* the best and give the opportunity for the fulfilment of the expectation and the realisation of the ideal. Forgiveness is experiencing in imagination the revised version of the day/event/person/reaction. It is to imagine and create that which you wish had been the experience. Not to forgive is to be in conflict and at war with oneself and the others concerned. Freedom and forgiveness go together. We GIVE the benefit and value that the other desires and possesses ahead of (FOR) even their awareness of having it, and thereby we benefit in turn. The Law of Assumption in action is able to engender forgiveness.

Forgiveness is to imagine and create that which you wish had been the experience, thereby granting yourself freedom from conflict with others.

It is the same as knowing that Buddhahood exists within everyone and remembering this when apparent circumstances make it most difficult. In Catholicism one beseeches God for forgiveness, and all responsibility is delegated to an external deity who arbitrarily bestows blessings or not. And how are you supposed to know what sort of mood he might be in? Only by the sort of mood you are in, obviously. Through a genuine understanding that we give to ourselves and others, the truth and circumstance as we would wish it to be, we assume responsibility and realise the freedom that this autonomy provides. The belief that we are dependent on an external superior power inevitably produces fear and anxiety because it isolates and debilitates us. Forgiveness involves a change of heart which is also a change of mind because the heart has a brain of its own, quite literally.[19] This, again, is a description of human transformation.

> "When we change, the world changes. The key to all change is in our inner transformation – a change in our hearts and minds. This is human revolution. We all have the power to change. When we realise this truth of life, we can bring forth that power anywhere, anytime and in any situation."[20]

This perception, awareness and attitude will not suddenly descend upon us in the hour of our death. We

19 See chapter 4

20 Daisaku Ikeda – On Attaining Buddhahood in this Lifetime

are far more likely to be gripped by fear and resistance unless we have practised the art of forgiveness during our lives along with insight into the true nature of prayer and faith – the potential transformation of denial into acceptance. Then we can be better equipped to approach death without embarrassment or any form of delusional performance.

Savitri (extract)

Yet in the exact Inconscient's stark conceit,
In the casual error of the world's ignorance
A plan, a hidden Intelligence is glimpsed.
There is a purpose in each stumble and fall;
Nature's most careless lolling is a pose
Preparing some forward step, some deep result.
Ingenious notes plugged into a motived score,
These million discords dot the harmonious theme
Of the evolution's huge orchestral dance

Sri Aurobindo

CHAPTER 2

PERCEPTION

If we accept that death can and ought to be prepared for during life, and not just towards the end of it, then it stands to reason that our various behavioural habits need to be addressed as they will determine the way in which we approach and experience death. I have suggested that much of the way in which we live is a form of performance, and in *The Alchemy of Performance Anxiety* this is described and explained as an idea in some detail. To recap briefly, the nature of performance is a series of decisions about how and what we present of ourselves in any situation, including being alone. It is not simply a set of reactions, but rather an attitude, a perception, and possibly a belief system, although not necessarily. As we perform in life so we might perform in death and, therefore, we would do well to rehearse. This is true for the dying process as well as for the psychic journey through the bardos after death which will be discussed below. Furthermore, just as in life, we must be capable and ready to cope with the unexpected. However thoroughly we prepare for a musical or theatrical performance, we cannot know absolutely that it will proceed as planned. There are so many variables that to contemplate them can only result in extreme anxiety, making it a futile and thankless task which would never be our aim. What we aspire to is an inner condition or state upon which we can rely in all circumstances:

> *"What then, is that state? We can describe it as liberation, transcendence, pure connection, and more. Meditation enables us to practise occupying that state at will, without musical instruments or scores. The benefit is gradually felt in daily life through our changing reactions, increased tolerance, and our ability to deal with situations calmly. We must be clear about what it is we are aspiring to in performance. It is not marvellous technique; technique doesn't communicate and cannot be addressed in performance – that work is done. Rather, it is all of the above – pure connection, and the transcendence of technique. In performance we are, essentially, meditating: highly alert and feeling part of the greater whole."* [21]

The art of observation is the practice of watching oneself think and becoming increasingly more identified with the watcher than the thinker. As this state becomes integral to our way of life both as

---

21 Clare Hogan – ibid.

perception and *experience*, it need never desert us under any circumstance, including death. It becomes our capacity to react to and deal with events rather than an attempt to determine and control them. There can be a certain security in *not* knowing, in embracing the mystery and relaxing the grasping mind's need to think it 'knows'.

In his book, *Preparing to Die,* Andrew Holecek discusses the notion of a 'good death' and is open as to what this might, but crucially shouldn't, mean. In fact, he suggests avoiding the concept of *should* altogether and advocates bringing 'the confidence born from preparation [to] let the situation, and the dying person, guide you'. He then quotes Joan Halifax who had worked with the dying for over thirty years. She discusses the concept of a 'good death' and her words resonate deeply with the idea of performance:

> "Our expectations of how someone should die can give rise to subtle or direct coerciveness. *No one wants to be judged for how well she dies!*" (My italics).

The expectations of others can be troubling in life at all levels of human performance and it's an understatement to say that we surely don't deserve it in death. This is a potentially contentious issue depending on family guilt, resentment, and blame. Although I do not intend to explore that especially, I do wish to discuss how even those emotional landmines can be prepared for and coped with. For that I will return to the concept of occupying a state as mentioned above – the cultivation of an inner condition upon which we can always depend – and will refer initially to the work of Neville Goddard as I have done before. In his book *Awakened Imagination,* and in the chapter *'Creation is Finished'* he describes the manner in which man is able to direct his attention so as to experience in imagination a desired circumstance or state:

> "*We, by a series of mental transformations, become aware of increasing portions of that which already is, and by matching our own mental activity to that portion of creation which we desire to experience, we activate it, resurrect it, and give it life... To enter a state, man must consent to the ideas and feelings which it represents. These states represent an infinite number of possible mental transformations which man can experience.*"

In *The Power of Awareness*, under the chapter heading *'The Effortless Way'*, he writes:

> *"Because creation is finished, what you desire already exists. It is excluded from view because you can only see the contents of your own consciousness. It is the function of an assumption to call back the excluded view and restore full vision."*

Nothing is Created, Nothing is Destroyed

The *law of imagination* is how I will term the philosophy of Neville Goddard. It need not be specifically ascribed to him and, being a law, it needn't be ascribed to anyone, but he is the main source of reference here. Buddhism is not a belief system but a philosophy that can be known through experience. Alchemy is an art, a philosophy, a law, and can also be an experiential practice. Just as Neville Goddard writes that creation is finished, Buddhism states that nothing is created, nothing is destroyed. To understand the Buddhist view of death is to consider its relationship to life and its knowledge of the eternity of life. We have no memory of our life actually beginning, and we *mostly* feel that it won't end, partly because we don't try to imagine it given that we don't want it to. Indeed, it is very difficult to imagine non-existence or even an alternative one.

"If when wide awake we examine our true nature, we will find no beginning that requires our being born and no end that requires our dying." [22]

The law of the conservation of energy and matter in physics states that within any system all matter and energy in the universe is a fixed quantity and that only transformation from one state to another is possible. This is Buddhist thinking also, and Shakyamuni was teaching this law hundreds of years before it was scientifically identified. It resonates with Goddard's idea that creation is finished, and you can occupy the part of it you would like to experience through the power of your imagination. Having a belief in the eternity of life might alleviate fear and anxiety about death to some extent some of the time, but there cannot be the profound release from what we think we desire unless we can actually experience

22 Nicherin Daishonin Goshu Zenshu (Japanese Collected Writings) – Taplow Court

the oneness of life and death which places us on an infinite timeline. Belief then becomes redundant because we *know*; we are living it every moment. This in turn reveals the utter irrelevance of so much that might have been held dear and clung to through fear of loss. The absurdity of the concept of loss is part of the truth that can set you free.

> Knowing that life and death are one releases us from desire and allows us to know we are eternal.

Daisaku Ikeda:

"We can understand death as a state in which, just as sleep prepares us for the next day's activities, we rest and replenish ourselves for a new life. Viewed in this light, death is not to be reviled, but should be acknowledged with life as a blessing to be appreciated. The Lotus Sutra, the core of Mahayana Buddhism, states that the purpose of existence – the eternal cycles of life and death – is to be "happy and at ease". It further teaches that sustained faith and practice enable us to know a deep and abiding

joy in death as well as life, to be equally "happy and at ease" with both." [23]

This is not necessarily reincarnation, because incarnation requires a physical form, and the continued experience may not occupy one. The cessation of the gaseous envelope that constitutes the body is real and inevitable; cessation of consciousness is wholly illusory because it exists everywhere, always has and if it ceased to exist there would be no awareness of its non-existence. The relationship between the imagination and the physical world, between consciousness and matter, is how we learn to navigate the eternity of awareness and to experience it in whatever dimension might occur at any moment.

Distracted From Reality

The body can be and so often is an enormous distraction from reality. One has only to consider the many decisions that might have been made were it not for the dominance of physical reaction and need. The human egoic mind only knows duality, and its beliefs, opinions and attachments are everything (to it). To

23 Daisaku Ikeda – A New Humanism, Weatherhill, 1996

experience the navigation of infinity is extremely difficult because we live in a world of distractions and are distracted by our own physicality. This is the nature of our performance, and why we need to practise if we aspire to perform from 'the top of the hill'[24] and live in frictionless flow. As T.S. Eliot said, we are distracted from distraction by distraction; maintaining attention on a chosen activity is doubly demanding when we are surrounded by immediately available amusing diversions from without and nagging doubts and weak rationalisations from within.

That this is all strongly influenced by our perception – particularly of time – can be illustrated by the necessary imposition of deadlines, including the ultimate deadline. When students are given twelve weeks to write a dissertation, many of them will still do it in a sleepless final one. They also ponder briefly on what might be achieved if this level of application could be maintained. That example can be stretched to encompass a lifespan, and our almost mythological perception of future expectation and longevity. The psychologist and author Oliver Burkeman quite recently conducted an experiment among his friends

---

24 Hogan – The Alchemy of Performance Anxiety, 2018

by asking how many weeks the average person could expect to live if they were still here at eighty. This was to be an instinctive response, not a quickly calculated one. It seems that most of us would guess numbers far in excess of the actual result which is approximately 4000 weeks. One of his friends offered a six-figure number. The point of this is that our chosen or appropriated perception of both past and future hugely influence the value that we put on the present which is frequently overlooked in favour of the next distraction. We don't feel a strong enough need to maintain clarity because somewhere there is an assumption that we have plenty of time to fulfil our repetitive resolutions to live a better life. The fact is there is no time at all.

The spiritual teacher Samael Aun Weor, who taught and wrote extensively about perennial philosophy and universal Gnosticism, talked about the necessity for humanity to 'wake up', by which he meant the awakening of the finite mind to the awareness of consciousness. He ascribed the cause for this profound sleep as 'fascination' which is an aspect of distraction. It is all that preoccupies us in the physical world – our life-situations, needs, desires, aspirations, what we think we own and aspire to own and even the illusion that ownership is possible. We rarely pause to question the nature of this apparent reality, and this forms the level of our unconsciousness, our prolonged sleep. We have completely forgotten who we are – a part of the one consciousness within which the material world we know of exists – which has a direct impact on our attitude towards and experience of death.

Lucid Dreaming

We can learn a lot about death through sleep which is extremely useful even though often ignored, because it is so frequent and habitual. There is a daily opportunity to evaluate, develop and grow from the previous nights' experience. Instead of always dropping off to the chance encounters of the dream state every night, we can practise lucidity to such a degree that dreaming affords us another level of awareness. We can do this by engaging in 'waking up' during the day and frequently questioning the nature of the reality that has for so long been taken for granted. For example, we could ask ourselves, is it possible that I am dreaming this? Might I be in someone else's dream? Am I able to determine this apparent narrative? And, if I'm aware of this being a dream-state, can I enjoy it for the freedom that it seems to afford? Our three-dimensional fascinations/distractions are also dreams, and they can be challenged and questioned as to their validity and 'realness' so that we cease to simply replicate these occurrences during sleep. When we dream, we don't suspect that our physical body isn't present because we are fully immersed in the dream. A dead person may not know that it is dead; it is possible that we have already died – and yet, on we go. Inhabiting the internal world of awakened consciousness, and the state of dreaming, are not the same as each other. The internal world of conscious awareness is anything but a dream; it is the most awake and aware that we can be, and, from that place of abidance, our perception of the apparently external world shifts entirely. There may be no more dreaming as we know it. This is the development of self-remembering which involves repeatedly asking ourselves where we are psychologically throughout the day and questioning the nature of our reality through our experience. This process of awakening develops the capacity for conscious manifestation as well as for lucid dreaming.

"Lucid dreaming itself is a kind of bardo or 'in-between' awareness where the dreamer engages in aspects from both the dream state and the

waking state. You maintain the awareness of the waking state while sustaining the environment of the dream state... So even though bardo means 'gap', and implies something that separates, bardo yoga is actually something that unites... it bridges life and death, uniting them into a seamless whole. For an awakened one who has crossed this bridge, life and death no longer have meaning... these two disparate phenomena merge into nonduality. And just like the awakened ones don't sleep or dream, they also don't die, in the conventional sense." [25]

This gap known as *bardo* is the in-between realm that the mind enters at the point of physical death. This is a central doctrine in Buddhism, and describes the three dimensions of reality in terms of form, ethereal form and formlessness, and is known as the trikaya. The trikaya is defined as being the essence of who we are, an essence that is fully awake. Holecek describes death as being an involuntary journey into who we really are, a plunge into the depths of our mind, and suggests that if we study the trikaya in life we will experience both recognition and liberation during and

25 Andrew Holecek – Dream Yoga, Sounds True, 2016

after death.[26] In fact, the first bardo is often entered in the dying process itself. It is where the ego boundaries of the finite mind start to relax, and the identity of the separate self begins to dissolve. This dissolution is also an expansion in the sense that the individual mind gradually re-joins the one Mind that produced it initially. Just as the mind gains access to areas of the sub-conscious when we dream, as its limitations disperse after death it experiences regions of the Mind formerly unavailable to it. The degree of confusion that might occur will depend on the level of awareness and preparation undertaken beforehand. If there is resistance, anger, and fear, then it will be a painful and bewildering transition. If one is able to recognise what is happening and surrender to it, the journey through the *bardos* (which takes approximately forty-nine days, according to the Buddhist belief), is likely to be a pleasing adventure – something of a field trip.

Only disciplined thought and imagination enable us to embody higher states, all of which are just as real as those we wish to transcend. Our ignorance and fear of the future stems from ignorance of the power of the imagination and subsequent experience. Acquiring

26 Andrew Holecek – Preparing to Die, Snow Lion, 2013

the skill of mastering one's mind is vital to arrest its capacity to take control of us. As quoted in chapter 1,

"It is only what is done now that counts. The present moment does not recede into the past. It advances into the future to confront us, spent or invested... not gone is the last moment, but oncoming." (Neville Goddard).

The art of dying is the art of transformation, and the mystical meaning of death is to die to one state and occupy another which we do by completely submitting or *yielding* to it. If it is only partial it isn't a death, and we remain identified with current conditions. The total abandonment of those familiar conditions, however much we may wish to leave them, causes anxiety. Most change causes anxiety, and it is quite possible to desire and resist change simultaneously, which usually results in conflict. We could, instead, follow the path of least resistance, the effortless way, and recognise that all of the events and circumstances in our lives indicate the quality and focus of our attention and our imagination. We can deliberately alter this focus and assumption at any time, and this is the connection between the art of 'dying' and of manifestation. The effortless way may be the principle of least action, but it is action nonetheless, and it is psychological in that it involves imagination and assumption without effort. This is just as true for the preparation and experience of dying and death as it is in every moment of life.

The Value of Myth

Mythology can help us in our understanding and acceptance of death and dying, just as the Bible can, and indeed any and all religion can when properly understood. There are innumerable myths and legends just as there are a great many religions and belief systems. However, in the distillation of them all there emerges a repetitive story from which a fundamental and unifying truth reveals itself. Interpretations may appear to vary wildly, but the truth remains unassailable as expressed in the perennial philosophy (see Appendix 3).

> *"Indeed, only one unique and cosmic religion truly exists. This religion assumes different forms according to the times and the needs of humanity. Therefore, religious conflicts are an absurdity, because at their base all religions are only modifications of the universal cosmic religion."* (Samael Aun Weor).

To the ancient Egyptians the *Self* was far more than the physical/mental human being having experiences that form selective memories out of which stories of individuality and uniqueness are constructed. The Egyptians recognised divine, infinite selves arising from plains of consciousness which produce mental archetypes that provide us with dramas and parables depicting human and god-like behaviour together with *states of awareness.* As I have said, we occupy these states mostly by default, but it is totally possible to establish a chosen level of conscious awareness up to which we can ascend.

Myths are stories *about us*, about humanity, from which we can learn about any and every aspect of being human from the lowest to the highest realms of being. They embody archetypes through which we can gain insight into patterns of thought, behaviour and symbolic imagery derived from past collective experience and which reside in the individual and collective unconscious. This is the value of myth – the recognition and the awakening of consciousness through intuitive resonance with symbols unconstrained by language and intellect. The 'truth' of any myth is qualified by feeling and is personal and even private; there is no need to attempt to verbalise profound insight; it would be akin to boring another person with your dreams. If a need does arise to explain one's interpretation, then the personal truth has been conceptualised and ceases to be one. This is not to say that a hermeneutical attempt at some form of expression necessarily lacks validity; it may be of enormous value personally. That is the role of art after all, and it can be shared without claiming ownership of analytical achievement.

> The truth of any myth is found in how it makes you feel, and this personal truth can rarely be shared with anyone else.

Levels of Consciousness

The key characters on this invisible plain of myth are the eternal masculine and feminine principles and their representation of levels of consciousness:

Feminine = receptive = subconscious
Masculine = giving = conscious
The spirit = intellect = mind

The gods of the Egyptian myths are the archetypes of MIND and give form to the reality that we experience. In alchemy the mind is embodied by Thoth and he is, therefore, the intellectual father of alchemy. He showed man the relationship between consciousness and matter, and he represents the connection between the external physical world (without) and the internal divinity of the self (within). In Greek mythology Thoth is Hermes, the spirit messenger of the gods. Hermes is the link between mortality and divinity and is the foundation of the philosophy and science that formed the art of alchemy – the Hermetic Arts. The teachings arising from this are to be found in the Emerald Tablet (a foundational book in the Hermetic tradition) and are expressed as 'As Above, So Below; As Within So Without'. They are connected via the mind/spirit to express full and immortal potential. (This has a direct correlation with Buddhism and is known as *KU.*) In alchemy, everything has a relationship with, or corresponds to, everything else, all of which is unified by consciousness and made known by mind.

Alchemy is the understanding of the relationship between consciousness and matter which are connected via the mind. For this reason, it can be very helpful to consider the nature of consciousness from an alchemist's viewpoint because they understand the correspondence between the universe and the individual, and between physical, mental, and spiritual forces. They also apply the astrological connections with the energetic centres within the body, and know that the consciousness of the practitioner affects the outcome of a transformative process at a molecular level. Alchemical codes assigned physicality (the without) to the invisible concepts of consciousness and spirit. Sulphur, mercury, and salt represent consciousness, mind, and body respectively. Mind is an inherent power of consciousness and so these two are intimately bound together. Alchemists in the past have viewed them as being like lovers embodying archetypal principles of masculinity and femininity which, existing together, produce the physical principle of salt (body).[27]

> *"Sulfur is the soul, the consciousness in matter. Consciousness is the actuating cause of an individual life. The spirit is the mind, an inherent power of consciousness – this is our sulphur and mercury bound together – consciousness and mind. Consciousness, using*

---

27 This will be discussed in chapter 5 under 'The Tantric Path'.

the power of the mind, organizes and embodies thoughts, giving them a concrete reality which they otherwise don't possess. This is salt which in turn makes all forms of matter." [28]

Mercury is also associated with water, liquid, the moon, liquid metal, volatility, slippery femininity (skidding across a hot surface; quicksilver). In mythology there is a clear link between Mercury's mother Maia, Jesus' mother Mary and the Vedic god of illusion Maya. All have etymological roots in the meaning of water, and the illusory nature of a liquid that doesn't cause wetness supports the notion of mental trickery at high speed.

"Mercury was, and is, in all facets of study, always the water. The messenger and communicator standing between these two lands. Mercury bridged the gap between what appeared to be two separate worlds. The presence of Mercury, Mind or Spirit, unified and made what appears to be separate, whole, placing soul into Body – Mind into matter – immortal into mortal." [29]

---

28 This is a paraphrase from Kymia Arts, author and owner Avery Hopkins, Alchemical Mercury: Mind in Matter. 28/02/2015 blog.

29 Avery Hopkins, ibid.

An understanding of death must involve knowing (rather than believing) what it is that dies. This is where some insight into mythology, alchemical and Buddhist philosophy, together with the Christic Principle, enables us to grasp that the body (salt) deteriorates and ceases to maintain its form at which point it is either burned or buried and dissolves back into the earth. And, as with every other human activity, this can occur at various levels of conscious awareness. This is the physical death. We have now considered psychological and physical death, i.e. the mind (mercury) and the body (salt). In the triune nature of Being, consciousness does not and cannot cease to be. The truth that sets us free is *knowing* that we have the capacity to determine our experience (conscious awareness), and that death is really not the issue; we could have been determining our experience all along. For the materialists, death is akin to changing cars; presumably you want to upgrade in order to have what you consider to be an easier, more comfortable and enjoyable ride.

Evidence and examples are always needed to support suggestions such as these. A few experiences are certainly appropriate here in order to validate some of these postulations and theories. Birth and death are the duality. Life is life and just is, as an energetic and invincible force. The question to address is: how do we 'make more life'? How do we create anything so as to experience it? Why do we want to? What is the nature of the energetic force that is the seemingly endless cause of manifested and non-manifested life? Examples of mythology, religion and philosophy will be covered by considering the Eye of Horus, the Crucifixion and Resurrection, and the Middle Way of Buddhism.

Myths and legends can be approached on several simultaneous strata and aspects of understanding – psychological, planetary, dramatic fantasy and history. These are all levels of interpretation that harmonise and dovetail together depending on the level of conscious awareness of the observer/hearer. (Myth as history; history as myth). An example of this is the opera *The Magic Flute* by Mozart. Children (and adults) can appreciate this extraordinary opera at the level of pure pantomime with glorious music all of which is accessible, pleasant, often amusing and always clever; and, depending on the production, all with superb visual representations. It is also a deeply meaningful allegory on alchemy, freemasonry, Egyptian mythology, and ancient initiation ritual set to music of extraordinary complexity within which mathematical conceits are ingeniously embedded. And it is the story of Isis and Osiris.

The Eye of Horus

This is the Egyptian story of Isis and Osiris who are brother and sister as well as being husband and wife. 'Set' is their brother and there is much rivalry for the throne which is occupied by Isis and Osiris and is the reason for them marrying at all. Set has a rather elaborate scheme for disposing of Osiris, but one which will make sense on another plain. He has a beautiful coffin made for his brother so that it becomes the envy of all and considered a treasure to be coveted. At a party to supposedly honour Osiris, guests try the sarcophagus for size in the hopes of claiming it, but of course it only fits Osiris perfectly. As he lies in it congratulating himself, Set nails it shut and launches it down the Nile to Osiris's certain death. It gets worse. Isis is determined to find the coffin containing her dead brother husband and eventually succeeds, finding it in the river weeds in Byblos. She manages to take it home and hides it from Set who, nevertheless, finds it in a swamp and in his fury prises it open and carves the body into fourteen pieces which he scatters far and wide. On discovering this atrocity, Isis searches for and finds all but one of the body parts – the phallus. Thoth appears and wants to help her. He fashions a golden phallus for Osiris which Isis uses to impregnate herself which results in the birth of Horus. Inevitably, rivalry eventually ensues between the adolescent Horus and his uncle Set who has taken over as ruler after successfully dispensing with Osiris. During one of their physical fights, Set gouges out Horus's left eye and smashes it into six pieces. Thoth later finds these pieces and manages to reassemble them almost perfectly. Isis has, meanwhile, been able to heal Horus's wounds which means that the eye from Thoth is a third extra eye and this Horus places upon the forehead of Osiris for inner vision, protection, and resurrection for them both.

Osiris's consciousness and what happened to him is the allegory for the fragmentation of consciousness which is the state in which humans mostly exist. Isis, the subconscious mind, the receiver and the manifester, is helped by Thoth/Hermes, the mind and intellect, the messenger. Through him she is able to gather together the fragments of Osiris and restore unity. This is a condition that we all seek, knowingly or otherwise.

"It is interesting to hold the Sun's relationship in mind to Gold when we consider the origins of Horus. He was the product of a Golden phallus with the divine feminine. He is a child of the Sun. The Sun being the central focus and the life- giving principle to all [is] why we see it associated with consciousness, the Father, the One." (Avery Hopkins).

The Crucifixion and Resurrection

The mystery of these two inseparable events are celebrated as Good Friday and Easter Sunday each year, but on various dates which is contrary to most other biblically observed occasions. This is because it is a cosmic event, determined by planetary movement and cycles. The first Sunday after the full moon in Aries determines Easter. Aries begins on March 21st and ends around April 19th. The beginning of Spring is when the sun enters Aries and the full moon will form when it is in opposition to the sun during this (and any other) cycle. These moveable dates cannot be anniversaries of the death and resurrection of a particular human being in history. They are not, strictly speaking, anniversaries. A psychological, and also mystical, interpretation of these events allows an understanding that the sun, upon which all life depends, 'crosses' the equator in Spring enabling growth and development of a multitude of forms including man. The crucifixion and resurrection mark the death of the old year and awakening of the new one. I have said elsewhere that if the word 'Lord' is substituted with the word 'Law' a clearer understanding often emerges. The 'Lord' is Consciousness, individually and universally, and Spring is a physical manifestation of awakening. It is the true meaning of resurrection. The crucifixion is a symbolic death and an example of the many deaths that do and need to occur in order to grow, progress and transcend from one state to a higher/chosen one. (There is an assumption that it would be higher, but it doesn't have to be). This will be discussed in chapter 5 when the understanding of reincarnation is investigated.

> *"The being who is crucified is your awareness of being. The cross is your conception of yourself. The resurrection is the lifting into visibility of this conception of yourself."* [30]

---

30 Goddard – Your Faith is Your Fortune, Merchant Books, 2015 edition

The law of assumption is an example of crucifixion because there is a crossing of two elements from which emerges a third which is the state desired. This is the nature of all creation: impression – reception – expression. As within, so without; above, so below – the potentially Perfect Matrimony.

The Middle Way

"Life is indeed an elusive reality that transcends both the words and concepts of existence and non-existence. It is neither existence nor non-existence, yet exhibits the qualities of both. It is the mystic entity of the Middle Way that is the reality of all things." [31]

The triune nature in Buddhism is perfectly exhibited in the philosophy of the Middle Way. The phrase sounds deceptively familiar and is not to be confused with the secular Middle Way Society or any other number of similarly titled viewpoints and adopted concepts. At the very centre of Buddhist philosophy lies the principle of the three truths. These are identified as *KU, KE and CHU*: non-substantiality which means

---

31 Allwright, ibid.

that everything is potential in its inherent nature of constant change; temporary existence despite non-substantiality and the true entity of life which transcends both and *is* both. This is Namu Myoho Renge Kyo.

This is the unification and transcendence of duality which is the aim and essence of the Middle Way. These three truths resonate with triune philosophy in other spiritual paths that also don't believe in an anthropomorphised god.

An aspect of human performance is the egoic drive to present a persona which adapts according to circumstance in order to afford (itself) the best advantage in terms of acceptance and approval. The Buddhist view is that people are neither good nor bad intrinsically; everyone has the potential to express delusion or enlightenment at any and every moment (KU). Dualistic thinking and reaction is what we are endeavouring to overcome whether or not we are aware of it. When we are in darkness or are deluded, the physically transient aspect (KE) is expressed as greed, consumption and grasping, which operates on an entirely physical level; it is completely self-absorbed. Psychologically, the need to be right, win arguments and intellectually dominate others is the negative manifestation of constant potential (KU). The obstacles to realising these delusions are known as fundamental darkness and are what we recognise as stupidity and ignorance. Ignorance provides a useful insight into the nature of this particular form of suffering: we ignore the very access to freedom from suffering because we lack the capacity to notice it (and therefore to implement it). CHU is the harmonisation and transcendence of KU and KE and is the essence of their fundamental non-duality. In Tibetan Buddhism a particular significance is attached to rainbows and the nature of their reality, the illusory nature of which is likened to ourselves, our thoughts and perceptions. There is nothing absolute about a rainbow because it is wholly dependent on several factors for its appearance and thus exhibits the interdependence arising from the philosophy of The Middle Way.

"The Middle Way avoids attributing absolute existence to either physical or mental phenomena. Both exist conventionally but are empty of absolute existence. Divisions are constructed by the conceptual mind and have no reality apart from these labels... According to The Middle Way, the absolute, underlying truths sought by

realists do not exist, and the search for them is as futile as seeking the pot of gold at the end of the rainbow." [32] (B. Alan Wallace).

We can engage with the performance of dying and death just as we can with the awareness of conscious manifestation; it is no different, essentially. By chanting Namu Myoho Renge Kyo we are able to activate a sound vibration that combines the three laws underlying all existence: Myoho represents two constantly alternating states – latency and manifestation – potential and transient existence. Renge is cause and effect and enables Myoho to operate. Kyo is the result of the myoho and renge; it is the link, the thread, the string of connection that results in phenomena.

'Simply put, all forms of existence, including the seasons, day and night, birth death and so on, are moving forward in an ongoing flow of continuation, rhythmically reverting back and forth between the two states of "myo" and "ho" in accordance with "renge" by way of "kyo".' [33]

---

32 B. Alan Wallace and Brian Hodel – *Embracing Mind* – Shambala Publications, 2008.

33 Tom Coujin – Online Forum Quora, February 2018

Knowledge from Experience

Following now are five separate examples of transformative attitudes towards death. They were first broadcast in the USA on National Public Radio in 2016 and subsequently released on BBC Radio 4 Extra in June 2020 as part of the TED Radio Hour (Technology, Entertainment, Design). Each of them provides experiential shifts in perception, reaction and attitude toward the subject and concept of death both personally and socially.

First is a woman who had suffered the loss of someone she described as a surrogate mother and, as always with severe emotional disturbance, she began to see the world very differently. Through a process not necessary to relate here, she created a community wall which invited anyone to complete the sentence 'Before I die I want to...' Even before she had finished enabling the facility people were enquiring about its purpose and were eager to contribute. Interestingly, none of the hundreds of comments were remotely negative, but expressed imagination, hope, plans, desires, and very positive anticipation. The 'Before I Die Wall' idea went viral and spread to countless other towns and cities.

Next is a woman whose complete TED talk is called 'The Cost of Hope'. She describes how she and her husband navigated his terminal diagnosis of kidney cancer and her main point (and a very powerful and pertinent one) is that the term denial shouldn't be critical and that another word for it is hope. The degree of unwavering hope that she and her husband maintained afforded them seven more years than predicted. More significantly, they were seven wonderful years that she counts among her best ever, and she rejects terms such as 'fighting and battling' cancer. They lived as many of us do, hoping for the best and doing as much as possible with their time.

The third example is an art project inspired by body disposal, a faith-free attempt to address the physical transformation of the corpse. The problem with burial and cremation is that the toxin riddled corpse pollutes the environment. The artist Jay Rim explained in her TED talk that we have 219 toxic pollutants in our bodies (according to the Centre for Disease Control in the US) which includes preservatives, pesticides, and heavy metals such as lead and mercury. Even the fillers and cosmetics used on the corpse for burial in order to make it look 'alive' add to the formaldehyde pumped into it in order to delay decomposition.

Apparently, this is known to cause carcinogenic and respiratory conditions in funeral personnel. She explored the possibility that we could be physically useful in death and contribute to the environment rather than continue to harm it; for human beings to create benefit, renewal and transformation at a purely physical earthly level by delivering our corpses as potentially regenerative sources of growth. Her answer is mushrooms. They are 'master decomposers' because they contain enzymes that break down organic material and decompose the body with high efficiency. 'Infinity mushrooms are a new way of thinking about death.' At a practical level, burial suits infused with mushroom spores are available to buy/order and request. The suit turns the body into a mulch which provides valuable nutrients to the earth. This is the cycle, the transformation, and a tangible example of the cyclical nature of birth and death. (COEIO.com)

The fourth example is from a Critical Care doctor who is often the first respondent in major accidents and thereby frequently has had to deal with patients facing unexpectedly sudden and imminent death. His learning through experience was that dying people prefer to have the truth than to be apparently comforted through false protestations of survival. He witnessed repeatedly the need for forgiveness, for remembrance and for the reassurance that their life had had meaning. He asserts that knowledge plus truth equals peace and acceptance, not fear and anger.

Finally, Dr. PJ Miller who is the head of the Zen Hospice Project in San Francisco wants to redesign the approach and attitude to death specifically through the redesign of hospitals which he describes as places for clinicians which, of course, they must be. His point is that they are dreadful places to die in or even to be very ill in and that it is possible to create environments that serve both staff and patients at an aesthetically higher level which would benefit all concerned. The difference between hospitals and hospices is that once in a hospice we know that death is the outcome whereas in a hospital there is some degree of hope. However, the fact remains that many of us still die in hospitals and PJ Miller's suggestion is that the sensitive and benign environment of the hospice could exist in hospitals which would enhance the experience of patients, staff, and visitors all of whom could feel supported and cared for. 'Let death be what takes us, not the lack of imagination.'

Paracelsus (extract)

TRUTH is within ourselves; it takes no rise
From outward things, whate'er you may believe.

There is an inmost centre in us all,
Where truth abides in fullness; and around,
Wall upon wall, the gross flesh hems it in,
This perfect, clear perception—which is truth.

A baffling and perverting carnal mesh
Binds it, and makes all error: and, to KNOW,
Rather consists in opening out a way
Whence the imprisoned splendour may escape,
Than in effecting entry for a light
Supposed to be without.

Robert Browning

CHAPTER 3

LAW

All transformation begins with an intense desire to change, and nothing can ever change unless the cause of our experience is recognised as our state of consciousness. This first step is often the most difficult and is why most people are incapable of creating the life that they want. Everything depends on our state of mind; it is the only thing that can be truly possessed and is the single most powerful force we have. Unfortunately, it is mostly left to roam wildly, absorbing and reacting to external stimuli in a haphazard fashion. This existence is wholly dependent on external events (which are effects arising from perception and assumption) of which we feel to be at the mercy. Inevitably, apprehension and insecurity are daily experiences when we are, (and *The World* is,) never sure about what might happen, but the anxiety arises from what our reaction might be rather than to the event. In other words, how it will make us feel, which is the most important aspect of life over which relatively few have control. Fear is frightening; ignorance *should* be frightening because it's the source of a lack of control over experience. To gain control, our state of mind and level of consciousness probably need to change, and this transformation begins with the desire for it to take place and knowing what we are hoping to achieve, and why. All people desire happiness, but the definition of happiness is obfuscated by connotations of excitement, celebration, and temporary fulfilment through activities and objects. All the time we believe that desire will be fulfilled and therefore cease, with the apparent possession of the person/object/substance, we will be on an endless trajectory of 'getting and spending' [34] – which most of us are. We are so deeply conditioned to live in this way that the very presence and experience of *wanting* can be mistaken for a form of happiness – the thrill of the chase, and on to the next thing. The actual cessation of desire is better described as peace; peace and love define the real meaning of happiness in western language and culture. Otherwise, we are simply describing relatively fleeting moments of pleasure. To live a life in which we contribute to the growth and benefit of ourselves and others fulfils our true desire for creativity and peace.

We can agree that desire is necessary to promote growth and development, but it can also manifest in ways that are destructive and misguided, in which case, as we saw in chapter 1, they are deluded impulses.

---

34 Poem – The World is too much with us – Wordsworth.

These usually end in remorse, or at least regret, and, for some, the very concept of desire produces an instant response of guilt because it stirs up notions of over self-indulgence, degenerative behaviour, greed, and *sin*. This in turn suggests suffering through punishment, whether self-inflicted or otherwise, and a sense that desires are to be overcome, denied, and transcended. Even a full-blown hedonist tends not to maintain the lifestyle indefinitely, but eventually feels the need for some deeper meaning and purpose. At the level of deluded impulses, desires still have a profound purpose and shouldn't inspire guilt; they are there to be used as a source of transformation.

"Creating enlightened awareness inside the human vessel is the alchemical great work. If, indeed, we want to change things, we must begin that change in ourselves. We must become the container for transformation. We are the alchemist. We are the Philosopher's Stone. If a million people changed themselves, the world around all of us would change. We are the magnum opus, the work itself. As our vision evolves, the magnum opus evolves, and the magnum opus eventually will create a new magnum opus. There are worlds we have yet to

see that we are building already through our daily actions, thoughts, and longing." [35]

Laws of the Universe

The laws of the universe have been adopted, adapted, and appropriated by many philosophical and spiritual practices. For example, there are the Divine Law of One and those laws revealed in the lost gospels discovered in 1945 and now in the Nag Hamadi library in Egypt. [36] There are the Seven Hermetic Laws of Hermes in alchemy which also form the Kybalion, the Mystic Laws of Buddhism, and the Laws of Attraction and Assumption that are embedded in all of these. There are many more, and there are also conflicting viewpoints as to their number which varies from seven to twelve. In this chapter I will identify and explain those laws that are common to all religions and philosophical/spiritual disciplines and then examine what they have to tell us about the process of dying and death. I will focus on the seemingly contrasting curricula of alchemy, Buddhism and Christianity,

---

35 Normandi Ellis – Imagining the World into Existence, Bear & Co, 2012

36 Appendix 1

although the laws extend to innumerable spiritual practices worldwide.[37] The twelve universal laws that inform many of these other practices are listed and briefly explained at the end.

	Hermetic Laws	Buddhist Laws	Gnostic Laws
1.	Mentalism	Burning earthly desires	As within, so without
2.	Correspondence	Illuminate darkness	Self-knowledge
3.	Vibration	Dispel Karma	Gender Unity
4.	Polarity	Buddhahood	Power of Assumption
5.	Rhythm	Removal of obstacles	No death
6.	Cause and Effect	Freedom	Abundance of truth
7.	Gender	No birth/ death	Truth and fulfilment

37 Monique Joiner Siedlak – author, Oshun Publications

The correspondences are to be found in multiple directions, and not simply imposed from left to right. They operate at many levels, and as we contemplate this chart along with considerations arising not only from the text, but also from our own insight and intuition, more of them will become apparent.

The Seven Hermetic Laws

1. **Mentalism.** *All is mind; the universe is mental.* The universe is regarded as a living mind which is shared with and connected to all other minds. This is why our thoughts are so powerful and influential in shaping our experience.

2. **Correspondence.** *As above, so below, as below, so above. As within, so without, as without, so within.* We are *microcosms* of the macrocosm – all parts of the same source. The interaction between our physical, mental, and spiritual realities is constant, and we can heighten our sensibility to it by developing our intuition and instinct so as to deepen our awareness of the interconnected nature of aspects of our lives.

3. **Vibration.** *Nothing rests; everything moves, everything vibrates.* Everything has a vibrational frequency, from the smallest particle to the entire universe. As interacting vibrating entities, we as human beings are creating and causing, with or without conscious intention.

4. **Polarity.** *Everything is dual; everything has poles; everything has its pair of opposites. Like and unlike are the same. Opposites are identical in nature, but different in degree. Extremes meet; all truths are but half-truths; all paradoxes may be reconciled.* The law of polarity is a potential gateway to transcendence, to experience the oneness and the non-duality that is the shared reality. On the physical plane we experience duality constantly, but that doesn't necessarily make it a reality. *All paradoxes may be reconciled.*

5. **Rhythm.** *Everything flows, out and in; everything has its tides; all things rise and fall.* The principle here is that nothing is ever still, but constantly in motion, in the physical world, including our bodies, and in the mental and spiritual worlds. It cyclically moves through birth, death, and rebirth

(in whatever form or non-form they might be). This relates to the understanding of impermanence, and to the need for being present, because it is always disappearing.

6. **Cause and Effect.** *Every cause has its effect; every effect has its cause.* Hermeticism states that we are each the cause of our experience, although we tend to feel that our lives consist of the effects. When we understand that we are creators of causes, we are able to determine the effects.

7. **Gender.** *Gender is in everything; everything has its masculine and feminine principles.* This refers to the different masculine and feminine energies, rather than to biological sex. The principle of gender is to be found in all things, physical, mental, and spiritual; it manifests on all planes. It is linked to the principle of polarity in that the apparently opposing qualities combine to create a whole. It is for us to balance them to experience this.

The Mystic Law of Buddhism

'In the innermost depths of all beings there is the primal life-force which causes living beings to live. The same force supports inorganic matter and works it into the harmonies and rhythms of the great cosmic existence. In Buddhism it's called the Mystic Law. When this force manifests itself in the physical world it appears as the laws governing the inorganic world which makes possible chemical compounds and controls the physical pulsations of the universe. In other words, the laws of physics, chemistry and astronomy are, simply, particular phenomenal manifestations of the mystic law of the cosmos. Similarly, the life-force constructs the world of spirit, creates intelligence, gives birth to conscience, gives force to urges and instincts and thus creates all variations of mental and spiritual activity. It's what is called god in other religions, but it's different from god in that it's perfectly eminent within the cosmos and in human life. It's not a force outside the cosmos, it is the cosmos itself. The true nature of the cosmos and of life is the fusion into entity of the physical law of life and the spiritual law of life. This fusion is

the process where life is created and made to spread out into the infinite.' [38]

The mystic law is the primal power within all of creation, the properties of which are as follows:

1. To burn away earthly desires that give rise to suffering.

2. To illuminate the darkness of ignorance.

3. To dispel clouds of karma.

4. To bring forth the pure life state of Buddhahood unsullied by the evils of the world.

5. To sweep away all delusions and worries.

6. To establish a brilliant state of absolute freedom that is never deadlocked.

7. To illuminate the illusions of birth and death.

Buddhism arises from and reveals that the supreme life condition of Buddhahood exists in each of us. This is our true nature in the perennial non-dual teaching. [39]

---

38 Daisaku Ikeda – Life and Enigma – A Precious Jewel, 1982

39 See Appendix 3

Our true nature can be defined as the essential quality of peace and fulfilment that we all share, and which releases us from attempting to seek happiness externally in objective experience. This quality arises from the recognition of our innate awareness which is constantly present and available to abide in. With this abidance comes the dissolution of separateness. It is a teaching that makes it possible for us to achieve a profound inner transformation – a transformation of our fundamental attitude and perception. That's why the emphasis is on the importance of what's in our minds, of the very nature of Mind.

For Buddhists, to base one's life on these principles is to exhibit the wisdom to deal effectively with any situation, creating the most valuable outcome. It is also to realise that one is eternal as well as phenomenal. Buddhists of all traditions engage in chanting mantras. The most usual mantra for Tibetan Buddhists is *Om Mane Padme Hum*; for Nichiren Buddhists it's *Namu Myoho Renge Kyo.* Chanting resonates with the vibrational world and affirms the truth and reality of the Law at several levels: the sound (vibrations); the intentional vibrations; the heart (brain/feeling) vibrations and the faith vibration. Faith **knows,** and what it knows is that I AM THAT, I AM. I am the

Law and therefore I am the creator; I am the granter of wishes and the cause of suffering. Throughout the bible we are told exactly the same thing. Substitute the word Law for Lord and the message becomes instantly clearer.

The Laws of Gnostic Christianity

Both the old and the new testaments contain spiritual laws that tell us how to live, die, and interact with the visible and invisible worlds. Much of it concerns giving and receiving, in the physical and the non-physical realms of existence. It applies this law to prosperity, forgiveness, imagination, faith, karma, love, and manifestation. Gnostic Christianity refers to the more esoteric writings and teachings that were edited out of the bible in the fourth century and which contain information and insights that reveal the full meaning of many biblical passages by completing them and making them less oblique.[40] To coordinate these laws with a similar and, therefore, comparable approach to Hermeticism and Buddhism, I will list them as before, although the list is my compilation from these scriptures. They take the form of sayings from the

---

40 Appendix 1

lost gospels, from which the laws will be aligned with those above.

1. The kingdom is inside of you, and it is outside of you. When you come to know yourselves, then you will become known, and you will realise that it is you who are the sons of the living Father.

2. But if you will not know yourselves, you dwell in poverty, and it is you who are that poverty.

3. Make the two into One and the inner as the outer and the outer as the inner, the above as below, the male and female into a single One.

4. Ask without hidden motive and be surrounded by your answer. Be enveloped by what you desire that your gladness be full.

5. Where there's a beginning there is no end. Happy is he who stands bravely at the beginning. He shall know the end and will not taste death.

6. To he who holds the Truth in his hand, more shall be handed; he who doesn't hold the Truth, even the little he has shall be

taken away. Be your Self, especially when approaching death.

7. What you desire has already come, but you don't realise it.

All of these laws are expressed through the prism of their respective philosophical and/or religious parameters, but are essentially proclaiming the same truth, which is expressed in the Law of One:

Creation is an all-pervasive intelligent energy that is both within and without everything that exists. It is all ultimately of the same one essence within many forms and configurations.

Energy cannot be created or destroyed; it is One. Within the One life, nothing can be lost or gained.

"All differences in this world are of degree and not of kind, because Oneness is the secret of everything." (Swarmi Vivekananda).

"A person experiences life as something separated from the rest – a kind of optical delusion of consciousness. Our task must be to free ourselves from this self-imposed prison,

and through compassion, to find the realty of Oneness." (Albert Einstein).

There is no doctrine or intermediary necessary to directly experience pure consciousness and to connect with the One Source.

All form (in the universe, in the cosmos) is part of an intelligent consciousness, and is a unique expression of this infinite energy.

═══════

As well as the obvious parallels with the non-dual philosophies of Buddhism, Advaita Vedanta, and Sufism (to name but a few), *The Law of One* also specifically refers to a series of five books published by Schiffer Books between 1982 and 1998. They were the result of years of academic research carried out by Dr. Don Elkins, who studied UFO phenomenon and extra-terrestrial intelligence. He collaborated with Carla Rueckert, who became the channel for a sixth density intelligence known as RA which is not an individual, but rather a unified consciousness group. The five books follow a question and answer format; Dr. Elkins asked them, Carla Rueckert channelled the answers and a third collaborator, Jim McCarty, recorded, transcribed and edited them. The book series has been highly influential in the development of various spiritual concepts, and widely referenced by many published authors and philosophers in a multiplicity of fields.

Chanting, Meditation, and the Law

As discussed in chapter 1, effective prayer depends on attitude and intention. By attitude I mean mind-state and the awareness that asking *for* something is futile because it reaffirms the lack of it and puts it in the future. The Law operates in the present tense only, which shifts the emphasis of prayer because it means that we pray/chant/meditate from the feeling (faith/knowledge) of having already received. We assume the feeling of the fulfilled desire and feel grateful for it. Ideally, this is a **conscious** interaction between the **super-conscious mind** and the **sub-conscious mind.** This is prayer, the knowing (faith) that we are creators and, therefore, must take responsibility for our experience. This is what is happening when we chant or pray; we *yield* to a feeling and an assumption. This works at the level of vibration which is the third of the

89

seven Hermetic Laws: *Nothing rests; everything moves; everything vibrates.* The sound vibration of chanting *Namu Myoho Renge Kyo* equals the combination of the three major laws that underlie all existence:

MYO = Latency
HO = Manifestation
RENGE = Cause and Effect

Cause and effect is the seventh Hermetic Principle and, along with the third law of vibration, it works with the sixth law which is rhythm: *Everything flows out and in; everything has its tides; all things rise and fall; the pendulum swing manifests in everything; the measure of the swing to the right is the measure of the swing to the left; rhythm compensates.*

KYO = The energy of connection; phenomena.

As suggested above, all form moves rhythmically between Myo and Kyo, in harmony with Renge and by virtue of Kyo.

Chanting produces sound vibrations, the strength and quality of which determine our experience. This is why it is important that the mind-state is completely accurate and aligned with the intended manifestation, and it never fails to work. Whatever state of mind engages in chanting, it will manifest as it always has done, with or without conscious awareness. This is the second Hermetic Law mentioned above: The Principle of Correspondence – As Above, So Below; As Within, So Without. Chanting can be and often is meditation; we retreat from the objective world and enter the real world of who and what we truly are. This second Principle of Correspondence is otherwise known as the Law of Attraction or of Assumption. The word assumption better explains the workings of the vibrational world in that it is feeling and emotion that create phenomena rather than intellect and reason. The physical changes that occur send powerful waves of information to which universal waves respond through *recognition.* Hence the importance of adjusting and setting the feeling state when chanting – and, indeed, at any time. Chanting/prayer/meditation is an intensely focused transmission and reception of a desired feeling state. Whatever it is we might be chanting about is only because of the resultant feeling that it will produce. To pray is to assume, accept and be grateful for the feeling of having received. At best, it is a language-free activity and barely an activity at all. Rather, it is an awareness of the awareness of what already is. This is an example of the inadequacy of words to transmit the ineffable. Daisaku Ikeda: "If you have a great challenge, you have to go to the point of victory first."[41] This is the law exactly, assuming the state of the fulfilled wish, fast forwarding to the desired conclusion, however remote and impossible it may seem, and dwelling there with the intelligence of the feeling state that it produces.

> To chant, pray, or meditate is to assume, accept, and be grateful for the feeling of having received.

Casting the Burden

This is a biblical expression with a psychological meaning (as are all biblical expressions.) The *burden* arises from the subconscious mind and is the cause of suffering both past and present – one is because of the other. The memory of the subconscious mind carries past experience which informs present reaction. To cast the burden means to relieve oneself of past misery which causes current unhappiness by

41 Ibid.,

sending it elsewhere, thereby feeling free to see and respond with clarity to any present circumstance. The question remains however, to where is the burden cast? Depending on one's interpretation, it is to the superconscious mind, that is to say, to the Higher Self, the 'Christ within', the one universal mind, the innate Buddha nature; in other words, to the supreme intelligence possessed by everyone that observes the thinking mind which lives in conflict between the other two. To achieve this capacity to 'cast the burden', we develop and maintain a steady relationship between these three levels of mind. This can be done through meditation, lucid dreaming, chanting and maintaining awareness over one's thought-habits and patterns. This is no different from any other acquired skill, and children are particularly adept at it, having little or no trouble with 'making believe' and thereby impressing the subconscious mind with the reality of it. It is the powerhouse; it never sleeps, it is completely obedient and will create anything programmed into it with feeling and conviction – *assume* you are that which you want to be and in that profoundly powerful emotional experience the subconscious mind will manifest it.

Consciousness creates our reality.

*"If I can deny the limitations of my birth, my environment, and the belief that I am but an extension of my family tree, and feel within myself that I AM THAT, I AM, and sustain this assumption until it takes a central place and forms the habitual centre of my energy, I will, without effort or thought, mould a world in harmony with that perfection which I have assumed and feel springing within me... whenever our assumption grows so stable as to definitely expel its rivals, then that central habitual concept defines our character and is **a true transformation.** You win by assumption what you can never win by force. An assumption is a certain motion of consciousness. This motion, like all motion, exercises an influence on the surrounding substance, causing it to take the shape of, echo, and reflect the assumption. A change of fortune is a new direction and outlook, merely a change in arrangement of the same mind substance – consciousness."* [42]

Everything in the world exists as an invisible wave of energy until we give it conscious attention.

---

42 Ibid.,

Consciousness creates our reality. The subconscious mind comprises 92% of the total brain and the conscious mind the remaining 8%. The subconscious has an almost perfect memory and stores all our sensory experiences for later retrieval which, in turn, determines our sense of self within our environment, primarily at an emotional level. This means that as human beings our experiences are the results of what is stored in our subconscious minds, and the energy of the subconscious mind is inexhaustible because it never sleeps and always functions. Nor does it give way to the conscious mind; it always dominates in situations of conflict or competition. Unless one's fundamental belief system has undergone a transformation, (namely evaporates), nothing that the conscious mind thinks might be beneficial will transpire. This is because the subconscious operates in an emotional and, therefore, vibrational field which cannot be overcome by thought and reason. When we passively allow the subconscious mind with its vast storehouse of powerful emotional memories to react haphazardly, we are victims of current circumstance interpreted by past events and sometimes trauma. Therefore, we suffer in our thoughts and feelings and unwittingly perpetuate this suffering through ignorance and complacency.

However, once we grasp the immense power of the mind and apply it systematically to re-programme the habitual energy centres of its subconscious forces, we are able to create and recreate our experiences. But we need to pay attention; it's possible to trample over a desired outcome simply by not noticing the details in front of us.

Language and Meaning

Chanting and reciting in a foreign language twice daily may seem baffling, but if we draw an analogy with music and our relationship with it, the capacity to appreciate and resonate with a language in which we may not be conversant is a fact that we readily accept and rarely question. To avoid the distraction of words and meaning at this point, consider instrumental music rather than songs. This helps to clarify what is meant by language. It is a vibrationally resonant soundscape that can be shared through mental, emotional, and physical reaction and response. No one needs to be a theoretically educated musician to appreciate and experience how certain music makes us feel. Indeed, deep analytical understanding can be an obstacle to surrendered emotional response and even a mechanism of defence against it. We often listen to instrumental music metaphorically as if to song. Musicians frequently refer to singing as that which they aspire to when playing, namely, to be able to surpass the physicality of the actual instrument and communicate through it with the immediacy of a voice.

Singers often have to surmount the potential obstacle of language whether vernacular or not. The constant challenge is how to make the text clear without sacrificing the sound, particularly because it is the use and control of the sound that conveys the *meaning*. This is true whether singing in one's native tongue or a foreign one. When singing in a foreign language we must absorb the pronunciation as it is spoken, saturate ourselves with literal and poetical meaning, internalise it to the point where we *are* it in order to express it at a deeper vibrational and spiritual level. Language works on intonation and rhythm to convey its meanings and it is this vibrational world that allows the meaning to actuate itself.

Frequently, we perform texts that need poetic and metaphoric translation before they can be truly understood. This is also true of chanting and reciting spiritual texts. The English translation of the Sanskrit requires extensive analysis and, just as a singer needs to internalise a text to be able to perform it with any authenticity, the Sanskrit needs a personal absorption of its profound meaning. Then, as in music (vocal and instrumental), one can experience an understanding that goes beyond linguistic analysis. There are words and phrases in all languages that express something so specific and culturally pertinent that a truly accurate translation is not possible. That's when we take an intellectual leap of understanding beyond the analytical mind to absorb a meaning that lies beyond the limitations of our own language.

"Every individual is at once the beneficiary and the victim of the linguistic tradition into which he or she has been born – the beneficiary inasmuch as language gives access to the accumulated records of other people's experience, the victim in so far as it confirms him in the belief that reduced awareness is the only awareness, and as such it bedevils his sense of reality, so that he is all too apt to take his concepts for data, his words for actual things." [43]

---

43 Aldous Huxley, *Doors of Perception* – Chatto & Windus, 1954

Hermeneutics is the art of making oneself understood through the language of interpretation *which has meaning for us.* We read or hear a book or lecture and absorb them at the level of contextual inquiry that we occupy at the time. This is why we can read the same book twice with a different focus of interest and barely believe we have already done so. It is also why our personal experience of interpretation can be so exciting; it is giving birth to a (seemingly) new understanding arising from the perspective of the input/source, together with our own search for information and corroboration and then a desire *to express and interpret* this perception and insight as it feels to be. This is the *felt* experience of knowing anything. There is no need to memorise data and quotations or have cue notes at the ready to support an argument. There might be a discussion, but nothing to defend.

> Truth cannot be verbalised but can only be felt. Art and music enable us to experience the expression of truth without language.

We think in words and use them to formulate our thoughts. What would our thoughts be without them?

There is an assumption that a greater vocabulary is more capable of expressing reality and, therefore, truth. But truth cannot be verbalised, and highly eloquent philosophers and scientists trip over themselves and each other through mutual misappropriation of words and meaning when so often they are actually in agreement about the fundamental issue under discussion. "Things are not as graspable and sayable as on the whole we are led to believe; most events are unsayable, occur in space that no word has ever penetrated."[44] Language is an intellectual pursuit whereas meaning is not. Articulacy brings us closer to communicating a sense of meaning, but it is the *sense itself* that ultimately matters. For this reason art and music enable us to experience the expression of an intuitive reality beyond the confines of words and language.

Dimensions of awareness

Thinking about our physical reality is easy because we have sensory evidence everywhere. Thinking about our desires is also easy because we can imagine them. Thinking about a desired state as a current reality is hard, because of the brain's reliance on sensory

---

44 Rilke, *Letters to a Young Poet*, 2013, NY Penguin Books.

perception for validation and proof. **IF** the brain can accept that the desired state already exists, it will work tirelessly to fill the void that has now been created, but it must receive the validation. This is achieved through feeling – the very physical and visceral experience of emotions arising from the knowledge that what you want is already yours. With repetition it then becomes 'normal' and is more like tracking a package online that you are confident will arrive. This describes how the Law of Assumption works and its effectiveness in its capacity for manifestation. The Law of Attraction states 'That which is like unto itself is drawn' which is a definition of the way in which it operates. Assumption intervenes and uses this law to purposefully attract that which is wanted. This is the art of creation – the consciousness of being whatever it is you wish to be, thereby creating a void which must be filled. Deliberate creation of voids is both the process and the application of this awareness. The law of attraction serves as stepping-stones providing feedback on our levels of consciousness according to our manifested experiences. It can be a means of co-creation, but it is the level of creation that we occupy that the law enables us to govern. The dimensional levels of interaction and engagement are quite different, and the difference is in the knowing.

Our beliefs inhabit our bodies at a cellular level; they cause our circumstances which in turn confirm them. The more real something feels to be, the more the mind will seek to validate it in tangible experience. This can be beneficial or detrimental. When we're giving our attention to things we don't like, the mind will search for more of things to support the feeling states associated with it. This is done to validate the feelings, hence the spiral effect of anxiety and depression. Because the mind is designed to fill any voids that relate to feeling states (which is the language of the subconscious mind), it can be deliberately employed to erase the unwanted ones and replace them with alternatives. By broadening one's parameters to create a 'new normality', all things are possible; any resistance is entirely from within, which is where transformation begins.

> Knowing that something already exists will make it so.

We live mostly in a three-dimensional world in which over 90% of our thoughts run unconsciously, based on the programmes that we have developed over the years. The nature of our seeming reality inevitably stems from the same source. The apparent time-lag between our thoughts and their consequences allows us to address unhelpful beliefs and elevate our conscious awareness. We cannot really imagine a fifth dimension but might be able to accept the possibility of one, where manifestation is immediate, and time is not a factor. If we could learn to ascend through the frequency bands to reach higher planes of existence, we would perceive a quite different reality or 'world' because our outer world is always a reflection of our level of consciousness.

In the third dimension we operate from the past to the present and into the future. In higher frequency levels time doesn't exist and parallel experience is possible in simultaneous timelines. A person can move to and from one timeline to another based on the vibrational frequency they are carrying. Most of us exist in the third dimension with the illusion of ego, time and space. This is the cycle of birth, suffering, ageing and death, relief from which comes from rising to higher frequency states and practising the art of staying there so that death becomes increasingly meaningless. This can be done through chanting, meditation, study, and teaching. Chanting is an active engagement with the vibrational world of creation and an acknowledgement of one's higher dimensional Self. This Self is the observer; it is the I AM THAT, I AM. Each time we chant, no matter from what pitiful third dimensional state we may be in, the act of chanting never fails to elevate our level of consciousness whether we have a focused intention or not. However, when intention *is* focused the ascent is steeper, inevitably. There is bound to be oscillation between frequency states as one becomes gradually more proficient at maintaining desired levels and this can also be experienced in meditation where such pure levels of consciousness can inform us more than any number of books and lectures. Many people experience levels of seemingly unexplainable intervention when they find themselves in situations of extreme threat and need that are beyond immediate possibilities of control. In these states of desperation, the mind suddenly expands to embrace assistance from sources hitherto rejected as absurd and non-existent, and the person is able to escape the immediate physical danger. That this default appeal to a higher order of control is not confined to a western guilt-ridden upbringing is an indication that it is almost certainly a subconscious acknowledgement of a greater Mind than the limited human one, and one that we all share.

The human mind is only one level of conscious awareness and so it is only one perspective of reality that we consider to be 'the world.' Animals experience reality quite differently; not more or less than we do, simply through a different vibrational filter. The term *'Mundus Imaginalis'* refers to the realm of the collective unconscious which lies beyond our finite minds. [45] It is the realm of the imagination, of pure, unfocused vibrating consciousness. As Carl Jung wrote, "There are unconscious qualities that are not individually acquired, but are inherited, e.g. instincts as impulses to carry out actions from necessity, without conscious motivation. In this deeper stratum we find archetypes, and the instincts and archetypes together form the 'collective unconscious'. I call them collective because unlike the personal unconscious, it is not made of individual and more or less unique contents, but of those that are universal and of regular occurrence." [46] When humans are awake the focus is narrow and seemingly personal. When we slip into dream sleep, the focus loosens and becomes receptive to suggestions far beyond the confines of our ego boundaries. As the mind expands it has access to

---

45 See Appendix 2.

46 C.G.Jung - *Man and His Symbols* – Doubleday 1964

realms that lie beyond the waking state and this is what we experience in some of our dreams, when we know that they cannot relate to anything we have experienced in our biographical past. It is as if we are either being invaded by another mind/dreamer, or we are not who we thought we were confined to, or both. *Mundus Imaginalis* is what comes after that. It is the realm of imaginative possibility and potential, from which archetypes emerge and to which some great artists, mystics and philosophers are able to gain entry thence to manifest it into the awareness of the human mind. Consciousness vibrates and perceives through a variety of filters, of which the human mind is just one, and the 'creative display' that it affords us is there to be enjoyed by all of the filters.

The Twelve Universal Laws

It will be seen that six of the following laws correspond directly with the seven Hermetic laws listed above: vibration, correspondence, cause and effect, polarity, rhythm, and gender. Even in the other laws listed, those of Gnostic Christianity and the mystic laws of Buddhism, correspondences can be observed between all of them, which inevitably reflects the Law of One.

1. Divine Oneness

This law states that everything is interconnected, every thought, event and action. It is the recognition that we and all things are one. The universe is mental and held in the mind of THE ALL. Everything we see and experience in the physical world originates from the invisible mental realm. This governs all outward manifestations in our material world. Through the power of mind, we influence our existence. What appears to be separate is actually all connected and thought also has an effect at an energetic level, because our mind is a part of the one universal mind and our reality is a manifestation of that. The underlying reality of the universe is unlocated MIND. This law allows a person to use the other laws to effect change. The awareness of our existence means that we are conscious and therefore we each create the world we experience.

2. Vibration

Everything vibrates at a specific frequency at all levels of existence, including ourselves. This is how we can interact with universal energy. The law of vibration states that nothing rests, everything moves, everything vibrates. The entire universe is vibration as is everything we experience. The difference between mind, matter and energy is due to the variation in vibration. For example, sound is light at a lower vibration and light is sound at a higher oscillation. Thoughts and emotions are also vibrations and the law of attraction itself is founded on this law. Understanding vibration and frequency and learning to control mental vibrations give us the power to have authority over our reality. The entire universe is a vibrating mass of energy.

3. Correspondence

Throughout the cosmos all things reflect and align with each other, on a microscopic and a macroscopic scale. As above, so below. As within, so without. There is no separation because everything resides in the one universal mind. The same pattern is expressed on all planes of existence from the smallest electron to the largest planet. The energetic and spiritual plane directly corresponds with the physical plane, and the energy projected by the physical body via thoughts, beliefs and emotions likewise correspond with the energy of the spiritual realm. This law enables a person to reason intelligently from the known to the unknown by using one's mind to explore the universal mind in order to address any perceived difficulties. There is universal correspondence between the macrocosm of all life and the microcosm of the individual; they reflect each other. Similarly, this is also true of our internal awareness and external interaction with the physical world. Correspondence is in all things everywhere – within and without, above and below, and it behaves irrespective of our knowledge of it.

4. Perpetual Transmutation of Energy

On an energetic level, everything is constantly fluctuating and evolving, and thought precedes all action which is why it is able to manifest our reality. Energy is always changing and transmuting into form and out of form. Thought allows us to interact with it to transform it into whatever we desire. Energy cannot be destroyed, nor can it be created. It can only transmute.

5. Cause and Effect

The law of cause and effect states that every cause has its effect; every effect has its cause; everything happens according to the Law; chance is only a name given to law not recognised. There are many planes of causation, but nothing escapes the Law. Every effect that is seen in the outside physical world has a very specific cause and has its origin in the inner mental world. This is another mutable law because the conscious creator makes the choice to rise above any circumstance that they no longer wish to experience. They become the cause that creates the effect they choose. They know that the law of cause and effect begins on the spiritual plane where everything is instantaneous. In Buddhism, the lotus flower symbolises the simultaneity of cause and effect because it flowers and seeds at the same time, just as our thoughts, words and actions immediately cause effects whether we are aware of it or not. This connects with the law of attraction, and we can choose to cooperate with it or to be a victim of oblivion. The Law operates with relentless necessity with or without our intervention.

6. Compensation

This law states that a person will always be rewarded for their efforts and contributions, however large or small, and often in unexpected ways. It is the biblical law of reaping and sowing, and directly linked to the law of cause and effect. All of the universal laws are interconnected. Where there is action, there is always an equal and opposing reaction. What we give determines what we receive. This can be realised in many aspects of life – happiness, good fortune, relationships, ideas and circumstance. It also connects to the law of rhythm. The key is not to view one's contributions as an investment, but to experience the benefit in giving and contributing for its own sake.

7. Relativity

This is the law of neutrality, which means that all things (people, emotions, experiences, and events) are only ever evaluated in comparison to other such things. There are always multiple perspectives on any of them, and our opinion, reaction, and perception (particularly of oneself) depends upon them. The law of relativity can broaden the isolated viewpoint to embrace the truth that there is always a person, circumstance or situation that is comparable to and better and/or worse than one's own.

8. Polarity

The law of polarity is the first mutable law and states that everything is dual and consists of opposites which are identical in nature, but different in degree; extremes meet; all truths are only half-truths; all paradoxes may be reconciled. Nothing is comprehensible or even conceivable without its opposite. The opposite of any perceived difficulty already exists as a part of it. In every perceived failure lies success; it varies only by degree. Nothing can be conceived to exist without the possibility of it not existing and as soon as a conception of that occurs, it exists. This is demonstrated in the reconciliation of paradoxes.

9. Rhythm

The law of rhythm states that that everything flows, out and in, everything has its tides, all things rise and fall, the pendulum swing manifests in everything – rhythm compensates. The ocean tides, business trends and cycles (art, opinion, fashion), life and death, creation and destruction and the swing in our positive and negative thought patterns. However far the pendulum swings one way, it will restore balance by swinging the other way. The act of chanting is highly rhythmic, and it is partly this that raises the vibration that also connects us to universal vibration of which we are a part. This takes us beyond our daily struggles and challenges so that we are not so consumed by them; we see them for the neutralities that they truly are.

10. Gender

The law of gender states that everything has its masculine and feminine principles; gender manifests on all planes – plants, animals, electrons and magnetic poles – everything. Men and women each contain their opposing/polar genetic qualities; each are potentially both. The masculine and feminine principles together are creative, productive and fluid. This means that while we all embody both masculine and feminine characteristics they are not fixed and rigid, but changing from moment to moment. For some this can be troublesome while others barely notice.

11. Attraction

This is the law of like attracts like, and the skill to making this law operate in our favour is to improve our awareness of vibrational frequencies so as to match those of the desired object, circumstance or condition. These frequencies can be activated and elevated through mental, emotional, and resulting feeling states. This is the art of manifestation. The law of attraction works by default.

12. Inspired Action

This law is closely linked to intuition, which means to be taught from within. It is to follow our instinct and make decisions to act from an inner sense of direction and guidance. This comes from a heightened awareness of the interaction of all of the laws and how they can be deliberately engaged with for the greater good of ourselves, of others and of the environment.

The Laws of Dying and Death

When contemplating the universal laws, whether in numbers of seven, ten, twelve (or more), the guide to translating their relevance and impact on our lives is threefold: that they are all linked to each other, that the source of the link is that of energy, and that they operate in physical and metaphysical (spiritual) realms. Everything, without exception, consists of and is generated by energy. The law of the perpetual transmutation of energy is one of motion and change; nothing stays the same whether it's seemingly physical or mental, but all movement and rest is relative –

another law inextricably linked to this one. Relativity applies to all things and gives them a degree of meaning through comparison, and the law of vibration is that of the comparative frequencies between different forms of energy, including mind and matter; the differing frequencies are all that separate them. The rhythm of these frequencies is evident everywhere – the tides, planets, bodily organs, seasons – the growth, decay, and cyclic nature of all life. As above so below, in the microcosm is the macrocosm, which directly connects to the law of correspondence, itself exhibiting the law of polarity. This law includes that of potential and balance, mirroring the equilibrium within the law of cause and effect and the idea of reaping what we sow. The law of gender reflects the creative principle which everyone possesses, of giving and receiving, which are not dependent on gender. This principle goes beyond gender difference and takes us back to the law of divine oneness and the interconnection of all things in mind, matter, and consciousness.

We have already observed that nothing is created, and nothing is destroyed. The energy in matter doesn't change, it only changes form. Also, all energy eventually converts to heat, whether it be chemical, electrical, or kinetic energy, and this remains the case even after death when all bodily energy becomes disordered and converts to heat. This is the process of entropy. Every living organism produces heatwaves, many of which are visible. There are certain house plants, for example, where the rising waves of heat (also referred to as the energy field) are clearly detectable even for the untrained eye. Whenever our body creates/converts energy for its various functions, muscles, and nerves, it loses an equal amount of chemical energy; this conversion is constant; energy is always being moved around from one form to another. This creative conversion ceases when we die because it is no longer necessary; we don't need the fuel anymore, but our bodies still contain a varying amount of it (the lack of necessary direction results in the disorder), sometimes a considerable amount, especially in the case of sudden and unexpected death.

So far, this is physical, measurable, and scientific. It is valuable information up to a point, but one of limited interest. Universal laws operate metaphysically also, and this is of greater relevance in the consideration of the dying and death experience. The energy of conscious awareness is inexhaustible because it is unlimited. We are exhibits of its creative play (mentioned earlier), of its manifestation in the innumerable finite forms that are the world, the universe and beyond. When we contemplate dying, it is usually as the singular individual that we imagine ourselves to be, and which will become no more than other people's conflicting memories. But all of the laws tell us that the infinite energy from which we sprung and of which we are a part is constantly there for us to re-join; there can be no loss. How long the sense of finite individuality lasts after physical death differs according to diverse philosophies and belief systems and can be anything from no time at all to forty-nine days, and on to eternity. This is the cause of much anxiety for many, and it is because the limited, time-conditioned mind cannot imagine a time-free dimension in which such questions are senseless. Universal laws embrace all of life – physical, mental, and spiritual; before, during and after corporeal death – and they are only identified separately because it corresponds with our imposition of disconnection to which we are so accustomed.

Human transformation is changing the causes from the past to reframe their effect on the present and the future.

Human transformation is a mental construct, a spiritual insight, and an emotional effort all at the same time. It is to fully change one's mind by turning any seemingly negative/resistant situation *around* in order to understand yet again that we are the sole cause. This is how karma is transformed, and it can occur several times a day in one who is fully conscious and awake. It is to change the causes from the past to reframe their effect on the present and, therefore, the future. To repeat from chapter 1:

> *"If you want to understand the causes that existed in the past, look at the results as they are manifested in the present. And if you want to understand what results will be manifested in the future, look at the causes that exist in the present."* [47]

Human inner transformation is liberation from the separate ego self. We can turn a situation around completely *in the instant of suffering*, and accept the truth concerning the effects of our personal cause.

---

47 Goddard – ibid.

Buddha in Glory

Centre of all centres, core of cores,
almond self-enclosed and growing sweet –
all this universe to the furthest stars
and beyond them, is your flesh, your fruit.

Now you feel how nothing clings to you;
your vast shell reaches into endless space,
and there the rich, thick fluids rise and flow.
Illuminated in your infinite peace,

a billion stars go spinning through the night,
blazing high above your head.
But in *you is the presence that*
will be, when all the stars are dead.

Rainer Maria Rilke.
Translated by Stephen Mitchell.

CHAPTER 4

BREATH

This chapter will explore the power and significance of breathing from the beginning through to the end of life from a variety of viewpoints that together should cover several aspects of the currently perceived human experience in the physical world. Our first intake of air is part of the trauma of birth and marks the separation from the womb which initiates a level of physical independence that we may not have wanted. That babies cry could well be from a combination of shock and horror. Interestingly, the first breath is an inhalation which is both understandable and obvious. It is less obvious that very often the final breath is also an inhalation. So often depicted and imagined as an expirational sigh of ultimate surrender, it is, potentially, both more and less dramatic. The last inhalation can be rather noisy which might alert a companion to the event because of the silence that follows.

Breathing is an activity which is mostly unconscious and controlled by the parasympathetic nervous system which takes care of vital organ function. Through a multiplicity of deliberate and consciously applied breathing techniques, practices, and disciplines, it is possible to achieve some extraordinary feats at many levels of human performance, giving us the potential to transform our apparent reality according to our intentions and desires. The performance and purpose of breathing can impact us in physical, mental, emotional, and spiritual realms, as and when we learn how to apply the required techniques and wake up to the powerful energetic forces that we each possess. These realms are not as separate as the list suggests; they all fuse and influence each other which will become clearer as we consider each of them.

> The performance and purpose of breathing can wake us up to the powerful energetic forces that we each possess.

In March 2020, The Shift Network hosted a Breathwork Summit over five days involving approximately forty speakers who are recognised experts in each of their fields. Day 1 was entitled *Conscious Breathing: A Treasure for Humanity and Our World* and included talks from Rollin McCraty of The Heart Math Institute (more on that specific subject in the following chapter) and Dr. Stephen Porges on polyvagal theory. Days 2 and 3 shared the title *Treasure Trove of Breathwork Modalities as Healer and Transformer* and included the Buteyko specialist Patrick McKeown, and the author of *The Art and Science of Breathwork* Dan Brule. Of the forty or so speakers, these are the people I am going to focus on here. They all approach and apply specific breathing techniques and practices for potentially profound healing and as a more immediate coping mechanism for anxiety, panic and stress.

All of the speakers acknowledge that the conscious and deliberate use of a whole gamut of breathing techniques has been widely taught and practised in the ancient past and is something that we have rediscovered rather than learned for the first time in recent years, as the title of Dan Brules' book suggests. At the profound levels of healing, breathwork is almost always employed to address aspects of trauma which inevitably involves accessing psychological and emotional states that might be partially or entirely hidden. We will discuss this later when considering the Holotropic Breathwork of Stan and Christina Grof.

The Buteyko Method

The Buteyko Method is concerned with the physiology of breathing and the damaging effects that inefficient (and unconscious) breathing can have on the body and therefore the mind. In his book *The Oxygen*

Advantage,[48] Patrick McKeown differentiates between mouth breathing and nose breathing, advocating the benefits of nasal breathing through the greater use of the diaphragm, the lower intake of air and the subsequently improved distribution of oxygen. This stimulates the parasympathetic nervous system which increases relaxation and calm as the breathing is naturally slower. Mouth breathing tends to be shallow, rapid and the cause of constricted airways and blood vessels. It activates the sympathetic nervous system which creates physical stress. It isn't the intake of oxygen that is in question; it's the subsequent distribution of it which is dependent upon how it is inhaled and to what area of the lungs it reaches.

Breathing through the nose rather than through the mouth improves how oxygen is distributed throughout the body and makes us calmer.

Deep nasal breathing opens the airways and dilates the blood vessels which not only results in improved delivery of oxygen, but also increases levels of nitric

48 Patrick McKeown – The Oxygen Advantage, Piatkus, 2015

oxide which is created in the nasal cavity. This gas relaxes and dilates blood vessels allowing better blood flow and distribution of oxygen to muscles and tissues. Mouth breathing is shallower and more rapid which increases the need to expel CO2. This creates a need for more air which perpetuate the cycle whereby oxygen is not distributed to muscles and tissue, but is retained by the protein haemoglobin, because a primary need has been created which causes breathlessness to varying degrees. Deliberate over-breathing through the mouth for defined time periods and for predetermined outcomes (intense physical exercise for example, or for some altered states of experience to be looked at later) are employed to achieve certain physical and biological conditions, but they are practised in the same way that any intensely demanding physical exertion is – and preferably supervised by an instructor.

It is the habitual unconscious mouth breathing that is deleterious to physical and subsequently mental health, as it is the cause of suboptimal endurance, fatigue, snoring, sleep apnoea (and therefore extremely poor sleep and more fatigue), throat issues, coughing and vocal side effects. McKeown's mission is to raise our awareness not only of detrimental breathing habits, but also of our blood oxygen levels and his method for testing this he defines as BOLT – blood oxygen level test. This measures the body's tolerance level of CO_2 and is done by counting the time a breath can be held after a normal inhalation before the first desire to breath occurs. He calls this first desire 'air hunger' which is not an attempt to hold the breath for as long as possible, but to notice when the natural need to inhale occurs.

The long list of physical malfunctions caused by poor breathing and specifically mouth breathing that McKeown identifies in *The Oxygen Advantage* is alarming to say the least, especially in children, because of the consequences in the future. He goes so far as to say that no child reaches their full genetic potential if they are using their mouth to breathe and he lists the reasons as follows: the air is not conditioned before it is drawn into the lungs; oxygen uptake is reduced as is the pressure of oxygen in the blood; disturbed breathing patterns cause a lowering of carbon dioxide resulting in constricted blood vessels and reduced oxygen delivery throughout the body including the brain; sleep can be severely disrupted with the onset of sleep apnoea, and craniofacial development is adversely affected because the jaw becomes set back in the face which narrows the airways as well as causing teeth overcrowding. Temporomandibular joint disorder (TMD) as well as being painful will also result in forward head posture which decreases the 'freeway space' between upper and lower teeth and increases pressure on the joint. Asthma, sleep apnoea, TMD, bruxism and a swathe of dental disorders can and have been treated with surgery, oral splints, orthodontics, CPAP machines, inhalers and general dentistry, but if the cause is not rectified by changing the habit of mouth breathing the results can only be temporary and partial at best. McKeown's mission is to educate young children as a matter of course in habitual nasal breathing thereby greatly reducing and possibly eliminating the need for such interventions, and optimising a child's performing ability at all levels – physical, mental and emotional – throughout their lives.

"Nasal breathing is the key to a child's development. We need schoolteachers learning about this. Why allow a child to underperform, to not reach their potential, simply because they have a habit which we as healthcare professionals have failed to address." [49]

---

49 Patrick McKeown, ibid.

HeartMath

Dr. Rollin McCraty is one of the founder members of the HeartMath Institute and has been researching the physiology of how the heart and brain communicate for over thirty years. The heart sends more information to the brain via the nervous system than the other way around and the quality of this information has a profound effect on brain function in terms of mental clarity, emotional experience and reactivity. By deliberately altering our heart rhythms we can influence the ascending information from the heart to the brain thereby creating the quality of our experience. In this way we can reduce anxiety and stress and greatly improve our health through the alignment of heart and brain. This is known as coherence and one of the methods for achieving it is through conscious breathwork.

Coherent breathing enables us to access deeper intuitive faculties and inner guidance which helps with otherwise problematic decision-making through a keener sense of clarity and vision. Our emotional states affect our heart rhythms, and those such as frustration, anger and worry cause erratic heart rhythms and 'incoherence' because the activity in the nervous system isn't synchronised; there is a lack of communication, and performance is impaired. Feelings such as appreciation, confidence, love, and compassion bring the heart rhythms into alignment and the subsequent coherence results in an overall synthesis of the body's natural internal cycles. What McCraty describes as heart-focused breathing can, with practice (and the practices listed in his book are specific, detailed and very accessible),[50] enable us to 'breathe into coherence' by modulating both heart and neural activity through attending to our emotional state and intentionally adopting the positivity of gratitude, kindness, and compassion.

> **Heart-focused breathing can reduce anxiety and stress and improve our emotional state.**

The actual breathing is controlled by counting and the usual ratio is 5:5 although it can be modified either way. (There are also many other practices with alternative counts that include holding the breath before exhalation). One imagines the breath to be

---

50 The Coherent Heart-Brain Interactions, Psychophysiological Coherence, and the Emergence of SysteWide Order – Institute of Heartmath, 2006

moving in and out through the heart or centre of the chest, and the rhythm that develops creates bodily coherence between the breath, heartbeat, and blood pressure. This alignment reduces stress, improves concentration, and has lasting benefits on heart-rate variability and vagal activity. Vagal activity refers to the function of the vagus nerve which is the 'wandering nerve' responsible for the parasympathetic nervous system. As we inhale, heart rate increases thus inhibiting vagal flow, and as we exhale it decreases with the release and return of parasympathetic activity. This is why an immediate aid to restoring a sense of calm when necessary is simply to deliberately extend the outbreath. Whatever our breathing ratio is at any time, it is always modulating the heart rhythm and, as we have seen, the heart sends information to the brain (at a ratio of 9:1 compared to the opposite direction). Therefore, to modulate the heart rhythm through coherent breathing is to synchronise neural activity and be in control of our own experience in mind and body.

The Polyvagal Theory

The function and activity of the vagus nerve was the subject of Dr. Stephen Porges' talk, also on Day 1 of the

Breathwork Summit. He is responsible for developing the polyvagal theory and is the author of *The Polyvagal Theory: Neurophysiological Foundations of Emotions, Attachment, Communication, and Self-Regulation.*[51]

The theory addresses the autonomic nervous system which changed over our evolutionary history as vertebrates, and as it did so it created different circuits to cope with specific reactions to circumstance. These circuits function in a hierarchy in which the newer ones are able to inhibit the older which were, and still are, circuits of defence. The most recent circuit is mammalian and social; it is how we relate to each other sending and receiving signals through our vocal intonation, facial muscles, hearing capacity and gesture. The pathway of the vagal nerve runs from the brainstem to the heart which, as we saw above, sends information to the brain constantly. It has long been accepted that the autonomic nervous system controls the sympathetic and parasympathetic aspects of itself, the first being responsible for rapid response to threat and the second for the smooth operation of the body's vital organs. Stephen Porges named his theory 'polyvagal' because he identified a third state

51 W.W. Norton & Co., 2017

that the vagal nerve activates in extreme stress or trauma which is also the oldest of the circuits, and it is the reptilian reaction of immobilisation when under extreme threat. It pretends to be dead. The key point is that this is not a conscious and deliberate decision, and when we as human beings revert to it we have not chosen to – the vagal system has. The body's intelligence has taken over any decision-making faculty that may be left under extremely traumatic conditions.

This has enormous repercussions in terms of psychotherapy, and also for the judicial system, because people are judged and indeed judge themselves for seemingly unaccountable immobility in the face of terror when the thinking mind assumes that the secondary circuit would automatically take control, and that 'fight or flight' would at least be attempted. The subsequent guilt and misguided accusation has been (and still is) the cause of even further trauma through lack of insight into human physiology.

The principal task of the autonomic nervous system is to keep us alive. The parasympathetic governs heart rate, digestion, breathing and organ function and is referred to as our 'social mode' where we relax, bond, eat and essentially feel *safe*. Physiologically, in this state our heart rate slows, facial muscles are activated, there is more vocal prosody and eye contact, and our aural perception is keener and more subtle. Obviously, the body's vital organs will continue to function when we undergo threat, but with a different intensity because there will be a rapid redistribution of resources including hormone release in order to cope with the sense of danger (real or imaginary). In that circumstance we lose any desire to eat and drink, chat amicably and so on, because there are more pressing issues to overcome. The hormone release increases heart rate and pain tolerance; facial muscles deactivate, and vocal tone flattens, while hearing focuses on extreme high/low frequencies. Our capacity to detect signs of threat to our equilibrium, which is always active and present, Porges calls *neuroception*. It never fully turns off, not even in sleep, but it can be impaired because of past trauma which can result in seemingly causeless trait anxiety through 'detecting' in the present something that really belongs to and stems from the past. This is neurosis (and more).

Breathing with conscious awareness can help us feel safe, which facilitates health.

The autonomic nervous system is one that links all body parts and organs via the vagus nerve which rapidly sends them information from the brain which has received and interpreted it through neuroception. It is also a two-way process in some cases, as we saw with the heart which sends information back up to the brain. The relevance of all of this to breathwork is that breathing is the only aspect of the autonomic nervous system with which humans have the power to intervene at will and at any time, and when we learn to take control of it the vagus nerve links the beneficial effects to the rest of the body. If we think back to heart-focused breathing, the cyclic impact becomes both obvious and hugely empowering. Porges' theory emphasises the human need for safety in order to live well and enjoy optimal performance. Feeling safe facilitates health and releases beneficial hormones such as oxytocin; it aids learning, critical thinking and productivity and it improves enjoyable social interaction along with supporting bodily functions, all of which human beings need to experience a fulfilling life. The portal to being in any sort of control is knowing how to breathe with conscious awareness when necessary.

Breath Therapy

Dan Brule is the founder of Breath Therapy and he travels the world conducting research, training people in breathwork and teaching the extraordinary benefits that it has to offer. He also emphasises the intelligent influence of the heart on the lungs which are 'wrapped around it' as he puts it. He connects breathing to creativity in this way by explaining that, as we breathe, we can deliberately awaken heart and body intelligence and consciously apply it to any aspect of our experience that we choose to, and that there is no domain of human activity that cannot benefit from this.

He points out what Breath Therapy is *not*: it is not a religion; it is not psychotherapy and it isn't hypnosis, even though it can be used for spiritual, psychological and remedial growth and development. It is also used for sports of all descriptions to improve athletic performance and indeed any level of performance in the overtly creative arts and elsewhere (think of surgeons for example). 'Breathing is the creative *spirit* in us. It is the language of the soul.' [52]

52 Dan Brule – Just Breathe, Simon & Schuster, 2017

Every psychological, physiological, and emotional state has a corresponding breathing pattern, so that each time our state alters so does our breathing. The potential power of this is that it operates the other way around, which is largely what breathwork is (as we have already observed). If we wish to experience a different state, we can achieve this by altering our breathing pattern which is what the training involves. There are innumerable breathing patterns and techniques from the world over and knowledge of their efficacy, suitability and specific application in any given situation requires training and practice, but Brule is eager to encourage the process as being open and available to all with the aim of gaining personal independence as quickly and efficiently as possible. It is certainly not a sales pitch, but rather a pitch for personal and shared liberation. He describes this deliberate breath-alteration, which affects heart-rate variability, as being like a switch or a dial that can be turned and adjusted according to circumstance (much as Rollin McCraty did). The body's chemistry can be purposefully changed by learning how to operate this dial. 'Breath is the tool of our day.'

We can alter our psychological, physiological, and emotional states by adopting the correlating breathing pattern.

Dan Brule also reveals some highly effective statistics, particularly those relating to bodily toxic release, and he does this to emphasise the power and influence of the breath. We expel a mere 3% of metabolic waste through defaecation, 7% through urination, 20% through perspiration and the remaining 70% through respiration. He explains the cleansing effectiveness of yawning, especially when immediately followed by a deep sigh; a yawn shouldn't be stifled but welcomed, and doesn't reflect boredom at all. This cleansing process occurs at metaphysical levels also; it affects the mind, the energetic body and the spiritual body as well as intuition. Breathing forms the bridge between all of these and is capable of synchronising them when controlled and manipulated through certain techniques. It is also the bridge between 'worlds' – the sub-conscious and the conscious mind and even the super-conscious mind – and it can allow us to maintain a constant awareness of these inner worlds and stay connected to them. It can also help us to strengthen the connection with each other which can occur in meditation, singing and chanting.

Breathwork is able to access and enhance the function of both the mind and the body and is a holistic approach to being human. It's a method of self-regulation and self-empowerment and enables us to discover and explore our highest potential and become liberated from buried childhood trauma which so often inhibits it. Women are taught breathing techniques in order to assist in the delivery of a human being about to take its first breath, and it is poignant to reflect on the respiratory effort that mother and baby both share during this powerful ordeal.

Breath Training for Health

Dan Brule was in the US Navy during the Vietnam War as an emergency rescue specialist who trained others in CPR, EMTs and other emergency responses as well as being a deep-sea diver and part of an elite team of diving technicians who shared the highest levels of fitness in the military. All of this and more contributed to his personal path of breathwork and to developing the first stress and coping program for the American Red Cross and to designing a Masters' program called 'The Breath as a Tool for Health, Growth and Change'. Deep sea diving was also the trigger for investigative journalist James

Nestor who was asked to cover the World Free-Diving Championship in Greece in which athletes challenge each other over how deep they can dive on a single breath, and therefore how long they can stay under and then return in a conscious state. He witnessed people going without air for up to twelve minutes and descending to over 300 feet, and these extraordinary feats inspired the research that followed, culminating in his book, *Breath: The New Science of a lost Art.*[53]

> *"The freedivers told me that... their transformation was a matter of training; they'd coaxed their lungs to work harder, to tap the pulmonary capabilities that the rest of us ignore. They insisted they weren't special. Anyone in reasonable health willing to put in the hours could dive to 100, 200 or even 300 feet. It didn't matter how old you were, how much you weighed, or what your genetic make-up was. To freedive, they said, all anyone had to do was master the art of breathing. To them, breathing wasn't an unconscious act; it wasn't something*

---

53 James Nestor – Breath: the New Science of a Lost Art, Penguin Random House, 2020

they just did. It was a force, a medicine, and a mechanism through which they could gain an almost superhuman power."

Nasal breathing can help us correct centuries of evolutionary damage resulting from bad breathing.

Nestor's book also contains many extraordinary statistics, particularly in connection with his research into ancient skeletal formations in animals and humans. He describes humans as the worst breathers in the animal kingdom, as a result of which we suffer from a catalogue of health issues besides the more obvious ones in the respiratory canon: blood pressure, bone density, cranial facial growth and dental distortion resulting from mouths reducing in size over centuries as our food became softer and easier to eat. Animals don't have crooked teeth and never did! Neither did we thousands of years ago, and nor were our airways restricted by a tapering jaw and an overarching roof in the mouth which can impair sinus function which inhibits nasal breathing. As we saw in the Buteyko method with Patrick McKeown, Nestor advocates nasal breathing over mouth breathing as our habitual practice and explains why and how nasal breathing has been so compromised through our evolutionary adaptation to progress. It seems we have indeed lost a very basic art and his scientific adventure explains where, how and what can be done about it.

Holotropic Method

One of the breathwork techniques that James Nestor explored and experienced was the Holotropic method created by Stanislav Grof in the 1970s. It is a technique that is seemingly totally counter-intuitive to all that has been discussed so far. It involves sustained hyperventilation which deprives the brain of oxygen, and which can induce hallucinatory states that are likened to psychedelics and 'tripping'. This deliberately intense over-breathing lasting from one to three hours is designed to stimulate the sympathetic nervous system to an extreme degree, and by extreme is meant a possible simulation of near-death experience. Why would anyone want to do that? Obviously because of the beneficial results arising from learning how to gain control of the nervous system and subsequently the immune system which in turn enables the healing of many chronic conditions, both physical and psychological. By pushing oneself beyond the stress 'boundary' and closer to the death experience, one learns how to return from it in safety and enjoy unbeknown release and relaxation. This is what is possible, and it can be part of the preparation for dying and death.

Dr. Stanislav Grof is a clinical psychologist and psychiatrist and is internationally recognised as an authority on non-ordinary states of consciousness and their usefulness in psychotherapy. He is a person who honours inner states of consciousness and respects their informative, insightful, and potentially healing properties. He is the founder of Transpersonal Psychology and of Holotropic Breathwork, and is probably the most radical psychiatrist alive today. He has been studying, researching, and practising holotropic breathwork for over forty years, mostly with his wife Christina, and together they have written several books including *The Holotropic Mind* and *Beyond Death*.[54]

He believes that the study of non-ordinary states is essential for understanding the psyche, human nature,

54 Stanislav and Christina Grof – Holotropic Breathwork, Holotropic Mind, Beyond Death – State University of New York Press, 2010

and the very nature of reality itself. These states are almost completely ignored within the academic sphere of psychiatry, and in the wider industrialised western world they are more aligned to insanity. This is because they produce symptoms that are usually diagnosed as being part of the cause and are therefore in need of suppression and control with medication and often internment. Ironically, it was largely through the introduction of psychedelics in the late 1960s and '70s that some of the more experimental psychiatrists were able to experience non-ordinary states which afforded them a western materialist's insight into levels of consciousness never to be accessed in a fifty-minute session on a couch.

The pioneering work of the Grofs since the 1970s has demonstrated that non-ordinary states of consciousness contain intrinsic healing potential which can be accessed and applied using the techniques within holotropic breathwork as developed by them. They are also fully aware that as a concept and a practice this is not new and that other cultures revere and aspire to these states as a way of life.

"The remarkable healing power of non-ordinary states of consciousness, which was known and

used in ancient civilisations and native cultures since time immemorial, was confirmed by modern consciousness research and therapeutic experimentation conducted in the second half of the twentieth century... Ancient and native cultures have used these states in rites of passage and in their healing ceremonies. They were described by mystics of all ages and initiates in the ancient mysteries of death and rebirth. Procedures inducing these states were also developed and used in the context of the great religions of the world – Hinduism, Buddhism, Taoism, Islam, Judaism, and Christianity."

(Stanislav Grof, Holotropic Breathwork).

The motivation to engage in these rituals and practices, and even to do so by ingesting certain plants and medications, may vary according to the underlying need and wish for a particular outcome, but they all share a primary desire to experience a different reality, whether it's for healing, artistic inspiration and creation, ecstatic union with another individual or with a group, or with the cosmos. It offers liberation from the 'skin-encapsulated ego' (Alan Watts) and the suffering that it can cause.

It should be clarified here that 'non-ordinary' and 'altered' states of consciousness are quite different, which is why the Grofs are always specific in their avoidance of the term 'altered' which is applied to conditions arising from pathological causes organically attributed to physical malfunction. The distinction is important in order to understand the healing potential of holotropic breathwork in the sphere of transpersonal psychology, which defines an understanding of psychic reality beyond the limits of biographical events. Stan Grof identifies these domains in three categories: archetypal, perinatal, and mythological awareness, none of which feature in western psychiatric treatment. Our model for therapy relies upon the stories of our early childhood, parental influence and subsequent misery inflicted by teachers, priests, and other sources of disciplinary guidance. No amount of talking, remembering, and reliving can change those circumstances; something else needs to happen and it needs to be experienced rather than discussed.

Holotropic breathing can help us access different domains in the sphere of transpersonal psychology.

As Carl Jung said, it is not possible to fix the psyche using the intellect which is only a fragment of the totality of the *anima mundi* – the psyche of the collective unconscious. This is the importance of art, not by or for the privileged and educated, but for everyone, and for those that suffer in particular. Truly great art is often borne from intense suffering through its capacity to transcend pain by expressing awareness of the collective unconscious and the oneness of being. Messiaen's *Quartet for the End of Time* is a towering example. Written in a concentration camp under the worst conditions imaginable, it remains a testament to the power and indispensability of art in all its forms.

Non-ordinary states function like a radar and find the areas of the psyche that require attention with an intelligence far superior to any that we in the mechanistic world can weigh and measure. Some of these *are* biographical; others are perinatal, and others are transpersonal.

Perinatal is obviously to do with the experience of birth, not for the mother but for the baby. We carry within us an emotional memory of our birth, which was traumatic. It wasn't necessarily the first trauma as we shall see in the transpersonal section, but in this lifetime it was. Perinatal means 'around birth' – before, during and after, and it is rarely a comfortable exit from one world to enter another. There is resistance, fear, pain, shock – trauma. And this is never referred to in normal psychiatric procedure, only partly because it is assumed that we don't possess the capacity to recall it. Holotropic breathwork reveals that we can and do, whether we know it or not, and it impacts our perceptions, reactions and, therefore, our experience.

Transpersonal psychology is an example of our capacity to occupy psychic realities about which we may know nothing intellectually, and yet we are able to *be* in an alternative realm or domain entirely. This is what Jung explained extensively in his work on the role of archetypes, and when his book *Man and His Symbols* appeared in the early 1970s it had a powerful impact on many areas of psychotherapy, and heightened the different approaches that then prevailed between his perception and that of Freud's, the necessary simplification of which (here) is that neurosis was either caused by (and possibly cured by) sex, or else an alchemical transformation of the spirit.

Stanislav Grof and Carl Jung are united in knowing that human consciousness functions independently of the brain and that an awareness of the collective unconscious means that there is only really one of us here. They are united in many other ways also; the power of art to access deities, archetypes and express trauma, and the capacity for the psyche to transcend and 'travel' way beyond the confines of the apparent present. At a physical level, Grof's work has developed from his research, with his wife, on the power and transformation which certain breathing techniques can produce. This is a transcript from an interview with Stan Grof where he answers the question of how he is applying his research to his therapeutic work.

"My wife Christina and I have developed a method which is non- pharmacological, but which uses non-ordinary states... Induced by faster breathing, powerful evocative music and a certain kind of bodywork in which we see the same spectrum of experience that we saw in psychedelic sessions, which is exciting because there is no doubt that what emerged from the introduction of psychedelics were and are authentic manifestations from the psyche. You cannot ignore what can be produced from breathing alone."

Trauma

The Grofs applied breathwork to access the presence and subsequent release of trauma being held in the body. Trauma and anxiety are not the same condition but, as I have already said, [55] much of the fear surrounding anxiety and its capacity to debilitate us is physical; we are afraid that our bodies will fail us and impair or even ruin our performance. As we saw with Stephen Porges' polyvagal theory, fear, anxiety, and trauma are felt viscerally and affect bodily functions including the ability to speak, remember, or even move. So much emphasis is put on our mental capacity to deal with emotional anomalies, but emotions are physical – they are experienced in the body. Feelings are different as they are a combination of thoughts and emotions and are experienced at a different level (heart-brain). As with every other form of communication, the same language is vital for any dialogue to be truly meaningful, and simply talking about past emotional distress and upheaval will, at best, merely grant us insight into why we react in certain ways; it doesn't alter the reactions fundamentally. Even to gain such awareness can and usually does take years which is both expensive and exhausting

---

55 The Alchemy of Performance Anxiety, FAB, 2018

– and doesn't alter the emotional field. Breathing is a bodily function without which most of us would be dead within minutes; it is also a potential portal into the psychophysical store not only of our personal biographical experience, but of the universally shared archetypal consciousness that causes and affects our interpretation of and responses to events.

Bessel van der Kolk pinpoints the reason why, in this observation from his book on the transformation of trauma *The Body Keeps the Score*,[56] "breathing is one of the few body functions under both conscious control and autonomic control". He explains the absorption by the body of emotional and psychological experience which may or may not be traumatic. The body will receive that which the mind either resists and/or cannot compute, and this happens without any conscious decision on its part. Along with Stephen Porges, he recognises the basic human need for safety, and that its absence is capable of causing a degree of physical paralysis extending to speech i.e. muteness.

---

56 Bessel van der Folk – The Body Keeps the Score, Penguin Random House UK, 2014

"Sadly, our educational system, as well as many of the methods that profess to treat trauma, tend to bypass this emotional engagement system and focus instead on recruiting the cognitive capacities of the mind. Despite the well-documented effects of anger, fear and anxiety on the ability to reason, many programs continue to ignore the need to engage the safety system of the brain before trying to promote new ways of thinking." (Ibid.).

Heart Rate Variability

Heart rate variability was considered earlier in this chapter with the work of Rollin McCraty and Dan Brule. To recap, HRV is the relative balance between the sympathetic and the parasympathetic systems. Inhalation stimulates the sympathetic nervous system (SNS) and heart rate, while exhalation decreases heart rate through the stimulation of the parasympathetic nervous system (PNS). These fluctuations represent health and well-being not least because they afford us a certain amount of control over our responses to events, because our physical reactions don't dominate and rule (SNS – over-reaction = lack of control). Coherence between breathing and heart rate allows some control over how we respond to difficult and challenging situations, and I have identified some approaches to achieving this earlier in the chapter.

As do several other breathwork practitioners, Bessel van der Kolk explored yoga as a means of synchronising heart rate with breathing and found that the holistic nature of the practice along with its wholly non-competitive philosophy enables a sense of self-regulated control which can be highly empowering. Yoga involves breathing practice (pranayama), postures, (asanas) and meditation, hence the mind, body, spirit connection which brings the elements of existence together in a coherent approach which can be conducted at one's own non-competitive pace.

> *"In yoga you focus your attention on your breathing and on your sensations moment to moment. You begin to notice the connection between your emotions and your body... you begin to experiment with changing the way you feel."* (Ibid.)

The word yoga means to unite, bring together, join. The treatment of physical, emotional, and mental health as separate issues has failed for long enough for anyone to realise that they are inseparable. Conscious and coherent breathing aligned with physical poise and control together with HRV awareness is the gateway to release from emotionally and therefore physically held trauma, anxiety, and stress.

Singing and Chanting

Another highly effective physical activity for uplifting the spirits, improving HRV and promoting controlled and coherent breathing is singing and chanting. I am both a vocal teacher and a Buddhist, the latter involving chanting twice daily. I mention this only to certify from personal experience the benefits derived from both activities, irrespective of initial motivation. With reference to Dr. Stephen Porges and his polyvagal theory at the beginning of this chapter, singing and chanting have a powerfully beneficial impact on the stimulation of the vagus nerve which wanders around the body supporting the vital organs. This support can be increased through the deliberate activities of singing, chanting, and jumping into very cold water. The resulting experience of making this effort is always increased energy, a much brighter mood and a sense of enthusiastic intention. They all involve an alteration of and a focus on breathing i.e.

it becomes a deliberate and conscious activity over which you exercise a level of control that is usually overlooked. Leaping into very cold water might feel and sound like an uncontrollable reaction to physical shock, but the intelligence of the organism rapidly adjusts the breathing ratio in order to deal with the extreme environment immediately; that's how you cope with it. (More extreme examples of this are to be found in the Wim Hoff method of breathwork which facilitates tolerance of freezing temperatures.)

The deliberate and conscious application of chanting techniques to address and heal trauma, epigenetics and ancestral family constellations is the mission and indeed creation of Jill Purce who is the founder of The Healing Voice, in which she teaches, guides and facilitates a form of overtone chanting that enables both singers and non-singers to access and release their voices which can result in transformation of the past and the future through becoming intensely present in this process of chanting. One of its empowering properties is the total lack of elitism often associated with group singing (e.g. choirs), where auditions are necessary, sight reading expected and a pleasing sound essential. She dismisses the subject of intonation by explaining the compromise of even-temperament and assures participants that singing out of tune is meaningless in this environment because you cannot be out of tune with yourself. Overtone chanting (which she studied in Mongolia and Tibet) produces natural and perfect harmonics above one's own initial drone. By accessing and altering the use of the resonating cavities, these inner sounds can be amplified and directed to induce (and restore) order into the physical, emotional, and spiritual body. This meditative use of the voice seems to be both an intensely personal and a powerfully shared experience simultaneously.

> Overtone chanting allows us to access internal resonance and restore order physically, emotionally, and spiritually.

Jill Purce's starting point in the 1970s was her awareness that as a society we had gradually grown quieter to the point of near silence which she attributes to advancing technology and growing elitism, both of which have the capacity to filter out those not able to compete successfully. The need to exert greater control always results in loss of control elsewhere. She identified this 'elsewhere' and set out to fuse and combine her two main sources of influence which were the western culture of educated elitism (she worked with Stockhausen for four years and was a part of his 'Stimmung' project in 1974) and the eastern traditions of communing with divinity through pure self-produced sound (she studied Tibetan Buddhism for decades). This became her mission – to learn from different traditions the potential of the voice to amplify the connection and relationship with a higher consciousness through the amplification of personal and communal sound (harmonics) without assigning oneself to a religious practice.

Chanting... creates a circuit of attention because you are doing the thing you are attending to. It induces order through self-tuning, reduces the boundaries between you and the group thereby creating a sonorous community of presence. This is true healing through internal and external coherence – reducing boundaries within and without.[57]

In 1984 Jill Purce collaborated with Marina Abramovich and Lawrence Weiner for an exhibition at the arts festival 'Forum en Scene' in Holland. They created a film called *Just One More Breath* in which Purce sits

---

57 This is a paraphrase of an interview given on May 20th 2019

in a medieval tower and uses overtone chanting on a sequence of extended breaths, during which the viewer rises up through the tower as time is seen and felt to pass from day to night, light to darkness. This extraordinary artwork of thirty-four years ago remains a beautiful example of the transformative power of applied breathwork which Purce continues to teach in her workshops and on her residential courses.

Controlled Inhalation and Exhalation

Another remarkable fact about Jill Purce is that she is married to Rupert Sheldrake who has been mentioned earlier in this book regarding his work on morphic resonance. This is the idea that 'there is a process which involves the influence of like upon like *across space and time ...* and that the morphic fields of mental activity are not confined to the inside of our heads' (my italics). It was inevitable that his wife's extensive research, experience, and scholarship on the application of vocalisation for transformative purposes would be drawn upon and included in his book *Science and Spiritual Practices.*[58] In it he

58 Rupert Sheldrake – Science and Spiritual Practices, Counterpoint, California, 2018

explores seven behavioural rituals that are commonly employed in most religions and offers a scientific validation for their efficacy. The chapter of interest here is on singing, chanting and the power of music.

Singing in particular, whether alone or with others, inevitably impacts breathing habits and patterns. One of the misconceptions about the importance of breathing when having one's voice trained is that it's necessary to learn how to increase air intake and to decrease its release. However, it is *the way* in which the air is inhaled that matters most, not how much. The in-breath needs to fulfil certain functions in terms of creating space, lowering and relaxing the larynx, and engaging the abdominal support muscles. This can and has to be achieved in a second, and therefore must become a deeply rooted habit at a physiological level. Most people over-breathe and do so unconsciously, as we observed in the research of James Nestor and Patrick McKeown on the detrimental effects of excessive mouth-breathing. As a demonstration to students and indeed a technical device to strengthen breath support, I may ask them to deliberately inhale (to achieve the conditions mentioned above), and then to *exhale* before singing a specified exercise. The sound is always clearer, intonation more accurate and it provides the awareness of how little air is actually necessary to sing a phrase well.

Controlled breathing and focused concentration along with the vibrational resonance experienced from within the resounding vessel (the person singing) all have enormous psychological and physical benefits. As we observed earlier on the stimulation of the vagus nerve, the activity of singing and chanting improves our well-being overall, irrespective of how talented we might be. In and of itself, it is not judgemental. The breathwork and the resonance don't demand a beautiful sound or perfect intonation. Rupert Sheldrake identifies three aspects of simultaneous resonance when people are chanting or singing together:

"First, with physical resonances within their vocal tracts and bones...

second, through the resonant entrainment of the members of the group with each other, chanting the same sounds in synchrony to a shared pulse; and third, through morphic resonance between those chanting in the present and all the people who have chanted the same mantra in the past, tuning in across time." [59]

Our response to voices and music begins in the womb which is also a chamber of resonance even without external influence. As intuitive humans, most people naturally respond to babies and animals with greatly increased prosody that would be deemed quite absurd if one was, say, in an interview. We instinctively know that the 'sing-song' high pitched nonsense that we contribute will be received at a musical pitch level of understanding that is neither taught nor needs to be learned. It could be likened to the cooing of lovers – crooning, purring gibberish, yet conveying essential information. This brings us to oxytocin, the hormone associated with 'love' and reproduction along with bonding, courtship, trust and the capacity to relax. The production and release of oxytocin is stimulated and increased by singing and is linked, inevitably, to the vagus nerve.

At the close of his chapter on singing, chanting and the power of music[60] Rupert Sheldrake asked his wife Jill

---

59 Rupert Sheldrake, ibid.

60 Ibid.

Purce for some practical applications that can be used by anyone. Her suggestions are a succinct summary of her teaching in this field.

> *"Most spiritual practices are ways of allowing us to be in the present moment, to be in here and now. We can only chant in the present, and if we listen to the sound we are making as we make it, we create a circuit of attention. This allows us to integrate with the unfolding duration of the now, where joy is to be found. When people talk of being disenchanted, I take this literally and tell them the remedy for disenchantment is to chant. To enchant is to make, and to be made, magical through sound."*

Singing and chanting help us stay present and find joy.

The Sheldrakes actually met at a conference in India in the '80s and both studied Eastern spiritual practices in considerable depth for many years. This affords them a deeply authentic and empirically informed perspective of the effectiveness and value of adopting any sort of discipline designed to uplift and enhance our daily lives. There is no shortage of advice on and offline guiding us to a stress-free, abundant and fulfilled life. If anyone engaged in a miniscule number of exhortations to 'do this every day to achieve your goals' nothing else would be possible, and nor would goals be achieved. Any meaningful practice has to be a way of life that becomes naturally incorporated into the flow of every day, much as mundane physical routines are. The most effective, transformational, accessible, and unavoidable of these is breathing.

Total Breath

Pranayama is the ancient practice of breath control in yoga. There are a variety of specific techniques to be applied for desired outcomes, all of which aim to achieve the connection between mind and body, which is the fundamental meaning of yoga – to join, unite. Without the inclusion of breath control, yoga as a physical pursuit is actually quite meaningless and has been adopted as a form of exercise in the west which ought to be renamed. However, there are practitioners, teachers and guides in the USA and the UK who embrace the philosophy and discipline of yogic breath control with deep respect for and experience of the effectiveness of pranayama on our overall well-being.

One such person is Dr. Richard Brown who, together with his wife Dr. Patricia Gerbarg, travels the world providing drug-free therapies to alleviate and even eradicate conditions including depression, anxiety, insomnia, and PTSD by teaching the application of breathing techniques drawn from yoga, Buddhism, Qigong, coherent breathing, and meditation practices. They are very used to responding to the effects of trauma in all of its manifestations, the most pervasive being the constant presence of threat, of never feeling safe. This condition is exhausting and debilitating because it results in hypervigilance and an inability to relax in the presence of others and often not even when alone. For some people there is no such thing as safety, which inevitably leads to chronic insomnia and its consequences. Drs. Brown and Gerbarg have observed people falling sound asleep while sitting up during a coherent breathing session because the synchronisation of their breathing with the other bodily functions, including brain activity, allows the *body* to respond to its level of exhaustion.

Coherent breathing and heart-rate-variability (HRV) were discussed above with the work of Rollin McCraty and Dan Brule, but it is worth revising it briefly here. Coherent breathing is breathing at a rate of five breaths per minute which maximises HRV for most people. The natural fluctuations in heart rate are linked to breathing and by changing the breathing pattern the HRV alters which in turn alters nervous system activity. Every breath we take affects our heart rate which increases as we inhale and decreases on the exhale. Through the application of coherent breathing, we are able to gain control of nervous system activity and increase HRV which improves the cardio-vascular system as well as the sympathetic nervous system. Drs. Brown and Gerbarg teach how to enhance coherent breathing with the introduction of resistance breathing which means to slightly arrest the flow of exhalation in order to increase pressure on the lungs which is actually quite soothing because it stimulates the parasympathetic nervous system, strengthens the respiratory muscles and improves oxygenation. None of this information is necessary in order to benefit from it. Cats do it whenever they purr. Moreover, the purring increases the state of relaxation and contentment, i.e. it is a cause as well as an effect. Recalling the work of Jill Purce, Brown and Gerbarg also identify singing and chanting as being a highly beneficial example of resistance breathing to which they add a third technique of *Breath Moving* which, together with coherent and resistance breathing, form what they term the Total Breath. Each technique needs to be mastered separately but can then be combined into a single twenty-minute or so daily practice. Breath moving involves nasal breathing in and out with eyes and mouth closed. Coherent breathing must be established first after which the imagination is deliberately activated by visualising the breath moving to the top of the head on the inhale, then to the base of the spine on the exhale. This is repeated for ten cycles and the whole procedure is called a circuit. In their book *The Healing Power of the Breath*, they introduce two circuits initially so that they can be incorporated into the Total Breath.

"Once you have mastered Breath Moving at the Coherent Breathing rate and you are able to perform it smoothly and without strain, you will be ready to learn the Total Breath. Each form of breathing we add to your practice increases the stimulation of the soothing, recharging, healing part of your nervous system. While these breath practices have traditionally been used separately, we combine them into one Total Breath practice in order to intensely activate the parasympathetic system and create the most powerful effects on the stress-response system in the shortest possible time."

They then go onto explain The Complete Practice which includes additional circuits involving movement, and the practice of meditation. Richard Brown studied Japanese and Chinese martial arts together with yoga and Qigong for a great many years starting in his teens. Later he also studied Russian fitness training, written methods of Systema training and respiratory practices from the Hesychast monks. In their extensive and ongoing work abroad including responding to several mass disasters, Drs. Brown and Gerberg are acutely aware of the need for disaster preparedness at an emotional and psychological level. The immediate response has to be rescue and physical safety, and the collective sympathetic nervous system has the capacity to achieve extraordinary feats in emergencies. It is the long-term recovery that can be easily overlooked, the PTSD with which we are familiar as a condition, but less so in terms of well-established drug-free procedures that require sustained treatment, care, and support long after the rescue operation.

Guilt and Grief

Among the most common sources of depression, anxiety and trauma arising in survivors are guilt and grief which frequently work together to cause psychological, emotional, and physical havoc. It is usual to consider grief in terms of the loss of the person who dies, but as part of our preparation for dying it is extremely beneficial to acknowledge the grief of the dying person which includes each one of us. Elisabeth Kubler-Ross identifies five stages of grief (denial, anger, bargaining, depression, and acceptance). There are at least three key points to make here. Firstly, that these stages are not necessarily linear and nor are they all experienced; that every bereavement is different and so therefore is the nature of the accompanying grief and sense of loss; and that the dying person encounters them also and needs as much support (at least) as the bereaved during this process. This is a form of preparation that we can engage with for ourselves and others if time and circumstance allow. We have already observed how the body absorbs emotional pain, particularly in the work of Bessel van der Kolk. Indeed, all of the breathwork specialists that have been considered in this chapter (and many more besides) use their knowledge of breathwork to address that very issue and apply it to heal and transform both the mind and body. This is why yogic breathwork is so effective; it is derived from the awareness of the powerful union that can arise from deliberately and consciously applied breathing techniques. The communication between the heart and the brain keeps us alive constantly, and our breathing patterns inform that connection. Of all our bodily functions, breathing is the one without which we will die most quickly – a matter of minutes. Therefore, the brain and heart can never cease to be in control and ready to respond immediately to any anomalies that might threaten our physical equilibrium. They are very finely tuned monitors and are capable of detecting the most subtle disturbances irrespective of their source both in time and cause.

The psychological and physical effects of grief and guilt are legendary and the purpose of mentioning them here is more of an acknowledgement than an exploration. It is the efficacy of applied breathwork not only to alleviate their damaging impact, but its capacity to reveal and subsequently release either or both as an underlying cause in need of recognition. Grief itself is not damaging; it is natural, normal, and necessary. It is also extremely difficult to cope with both for the griever and those around them. As a society and a culture, we are short on ritual to demonstrate emotional pain and ill at ease when faced with it, whether it's ours or someone else's. We are, however, collectively efficient at denying it – not the actual event of death, but the effect of it.

There are myriad responses to loss, many of which involve action or, more accurately, distraction. Unacknowledged emotional pain becomes buried, often so deeply that we lose all sight of it and fail to make a connection when the depression and anxiety arise months and sometimes years later. Suppressed grief will frequently be included in the category of trauma and as such has been noted in the work of most of the breathwork specialists mentioned above. Max Strom is a teacher and author on subjects embracing breathing techniques, yoga, and movement, and he has made detailed observations on the capacity of specific breathing techniques to access and release deeply buried grief in order to alleviate chronic anxiety, panic and depression.

When someone with serious and consistent anxiety issues is questioned about the source, they almost never have any idea. It is a condition seemingly without a cause that might vary in intensity, but never really disappears. The fact is that they have long since lost sight of the cause and need help and guidance to access it which forms a significant amount of Strom's work as a breathwork consultant. He enables people to reawaken past loss and engage in the grieving process which was formerly denied and/or ignored. Identifying and confronting the cause with the support of applying specific breathing practices, they manage to hold on to the control they have been so terrified of losing. As noted earlier, talking therapies are slow, expensive, and ineffective. Recalling that the body holds the emotional information ('keeps the score') and provides the experience of grief, it must be to the body that we turn in order to alleviate it, and breathing is by far the most direct and swiftly transformative route.

It is worth looking at the nature of grief in more detail to ascertain the emotional components that can impact us so profoundly. In his book *Preparing to Die*, Andrew Holecek introduces the thanotologist Kim Mooney who is the founder of Practically Dying and the winner of the International Association of Death Education and Counselling's Community Educator Award 2018. She contributes to his chapter entitled 'After Death' with a section sub-headed 'Working With Grief.' It is worth quoting a substantial extract from it to provide reference points for further consideration:

"We think of grief primarily as sadness and emptiness, but it is far more than that. Grief is alchemy – it cracks us open and creates opportunities for transformation. It insults the mind, taxes the body, and flings us into unpredictable contradiction. [Grief] upends our values and priorities and leaves no part of us untouched or unchanged... Our brains, which consume a huge amount of energy, are not our best friends when we are in loss. They tell us to think, feel and behave normally when we cannot. Then they shame us because we cannot... We add to the very real burdens of grief by imposing our judgements upon them and by accepting or imagining the opinions of others instead of trusting our own... With confusion and relief, we see that there is nothing absolutely true or untrue; grief unhinges our certainty about all manner of things... Grief is our human birthright, and it is our most powerful spiritual ally because it is embedded in the fabric of daily life and has the power to break our ego... Whether we choose to recognize it or not, grief is our messiest blessing." [61]

61 Andrew Holecek – Preparing to Die, Snow Lion, 2013

Trauma vs. Grief

It is necessary to define and clarify the difference between trauma and grief because they are far from being the same condition. Genuine grief is the opposite of trauma; trauma is the resistance to grief. Grieving is the process of gradually coming to terms with and accepting the loss. Trauma is the result of the many defence mechanisms arising from *not* coming to terms with it, and the cost of this is absorbed by the body and manifests in a dislocated form sometime later. Pain, suffering, and fear are all natural responses and not in themselves traumatic. This is because they *are* responses; they are an active expression of feelings about a given situation or event. There is agency and release. To experience a sense of helpless isolation in the face of a seemingly unbearable loss causing withheld and denied grief, which can continue for years, results in trauma. The psychotherapist Julia Samuel MBE who specialises in the subject of grief reports that 15% of all psychological disorders come from unresolved grief. "It is through grieving that we heal; when we block our grieving we arrest our healing." [62]

---

62 Julia Samuel – This Too Shall Pass, Penguin Life PRH, 2020. Grief
    Works, 2017

> Grief is coming to terms with loss, but trauma is the result of defence mechanisms springing up from not coming to terms with it.

She identifies guilt as being among the most painful aspects of grief, whether it's because we are still alive or that we didn't do enough, say what should have been said, expressed our love enough or perhaps we worry that we might have contributed in some way towards their suffering (at any time in the past, which can suddenly become alarmingly present when someone dies). One of her recommendations is to take exercise, which seems strange initially, but it relates directly to breathing which is so adversely affected when someone close to us dies. We are in shock, whether we know it or not, and, as we have observed earlier in this chapter, shock can cause us to freeze as well as 'fighting and flying'.

"Every thought has a physiological component, so we are in bodied beings as well as brain beings. Pain is felt in our bodies, and people often feel as if their heart is actually breaking, or in their chest affecting their breathing... Grief is a small tidy word that describes a very messy

*chaotic process... the pain is what forces you to
adjust to the reality that this person has died.
And pain is the agent of change. It is through
grieving that we heal."* [63]

These differences between trauma and grief are
important to define, not least so that we can consider
the best approach to adopt for both. If conscious and
deliberate breathwork became part of the grieving
process as a normal matter of course then potential
trauma could be avoided and possibly bypassed
altogether. Breathwork is an immediately powerful
tool in the arsenal of tools often necessary to enable
us to address and accept situations and circumstances
in life. It isn't so much what happens to us, but our
capacity to allow it to be happening without feeling
devastated and disabled.

It is utterly feasible to incorporate breathing awareness
and practices in childhood, in schools, as a short daily
routine, free from special significance and duty. There
need be nothing evangelical about it; it isn't a religion
or belief of any kind. It is more empowering than
either, because we all own our breath intake until

---

63 Ibid.,

we don't, when we either require assistance or have actually died.

Breathwork experts such as Stan Grof, Stephen Porges, Dan Brule, Richard Brown, and Patrick McKeown have done and still do vital work in helping, enabling, and liberating many people from the miserable constraints of trauma. Trauma is not inevitable for everyone, but grief probably is, and the transition from one to the other could be avoided with foresight, imagination, and compassion. It would also spare many of us so much unnecessary medication.

It's important to practise breathwork over a long period for it to be optimally effective in any demanding situation, including the onset of death. It is quite possible to gradually assemble an arsenal of breathing procedures that can be at our disposal to quickly and effectively access and employ, as and when required. It is too late to begin to consider coping strategies shortly before an event (performance); the necessary shift in perception, habits and practice need to have become a way of life a long time beforehand. As an example, simply by extending the outbreath and slowing it down we have altered our breathing pattern and increased the vagal influence on our heart rate thereby inhibiting the sympathetic nervous system. This simple technique is immediately effective and is used to control anxiety, stress, and performance nerves of all kinds.

The Potential of Breathwork

Human beings have the unique ability to intercept and interfere with their breathing and thereby access the extraordinary potential which is there for the taking, to gain personal, emotional and physical control. Emotions are experienced physically – that's how the body keeps the score – and the cycle of fear and anxiety which is so intensified through our physiological responses can be broken with the application of well-established and internalised breathwork. There's a breathing technique for any and every situation – all there for free. It can provide the space we need to accept the pain of loss, however long that takes, and stop it from sinking into trauma.

There's a breathing technique for any and every situation.

The transformative powers of breathing operate in the macrocosm of the universe as well as the microcosm of the individual; as above, so below. The philosopher and astrologer Dr. Richard Tarnas described this beautifully in a talk he delivered in November 2020 in which he explained the synthesis between Aristotle and Plato as identified by Plotinus, in whose view the stars are like a language that speaks from the deeper soul of the cosmos – the anima mundi – and that everything is interconnected and 'breathes together. The impelling stars breathe together'. The influence of synchronous breathing on a cosmological scale and its possible impact on the causation of consciousness is the subject of the next chapter.

No Coward Soul Is Mine

No coward soul is mine
No trembler in the world's storm-troubled sphere
I see heaven's glories shine
And faith shines equal arming me from Fear

O God within my breast
Almighty ever-present Deity
Life, that in me hast rest,
As I Undying Life, have power in Thee

Breath

Vain are the thousand creeds
That move men's hearts, unutterably vain,
Worthless as withered weeds
Or idlest froth amid the boundless main

To waken doubt in one
Holding so fast by thy infinity,
So surely anchored on
The steadfast rock of Immortality.

With wide-embracing love
Thy spirit animates eternal years
Pervades and broods above,
Changes, sustains, dissolves, creates and rears

Though earth and moon were gone
And suns and universes ceased to be
And though wert left alone
Every Existence would exist in thee

There is not room for Death
Nor atom that his might could render void
Since thou art Being and Breath
And what thou art may never be destroyed.

Emily Brontë

CHAPTER 5

PURPOSE

When we consider the nature of causality it is necessary to differentiate between a mechanistic viewpoint and one of conscious awareness. The mechanistic world view, which really began with Descartes, explains the whole of nature according to mechanical laws – the arrangement and movement of specified parts, including the brain. Conscious awareness stems from an experiential perspective which reaches far beyond the finite operations of the mechanical world which is considered to be functional but egregiously limited. The law of cause and effect presupposes the existence of a cause. Now we will consider the source and nature of cause, i.e. what causes cause? This also necessitates consideration of the impact of astrology, because of the duality between feeling and/or believing that our connection with the cosmos predetermines the trajectory of our lives, or that we, as an integral part of the 'breathing together' universe, have agency over our experience through conscious awareness and our capacity to harness and interact with the holistic nature of the law. The 'billiard ball' analogy of causality illustrates the mechanistic view of linear reasoning – one thing occurs because another just made it happen (and it is visible). Becoming more consciously aware helps us move beyond this mechanistic viewpoint. As I have observed elsewhere when discussing alchemy, the consciousness of the practitioner is the key component in terms of outcome whether it be a spagyric, [64] a glass of water or a coincidence.

A synchronicity ('at the same time') is a coincidence with *meaning and significance* both on an individual level and on a cosmological one. They are not separate and nor can they be. Our conscious awareness (of itself) enables us to interact with both the macrocosm and the microcosm (the latter being that to which we erroneously believe ourselves to be limited) and therefore to determine the nature of our experience. And this is all that we really desire – to be in control of our happiness.

Human 'Dethronement'

A spiritual emergency, as identified by Stanislav Grof, is an eruption of unconscious material which is unavoidable, hence the emergency. There is a loss of identity and sense of reality which inevitably results in extreme uncertainty. This crisis of meaning is necessary for any moral transformation to take place

---

64 A spagyric is the result arising from the alchemical procedure of extraction and distillation.

on an individual, societal, and even on a global level. From a certain perspective, we all might be currently experiencing a form of near-death experience which is well known to cause a major reconfiguration of value and meaning for anyone who undergoes it. This form of NDE is not the physical death that many are suffering from, but the collective dying to a state in order to transform into another, more enlightened one. We need to die to our former habits and assumptions if the species and the planet are to survive, and not just survive, but flourish. The planet probably will, but human beings may not for very much longer.

Humans are undergoing a spiritual emergency during climate change.

It has been said that human beings are going through a period of 'dethronement', having to learn that we are not the only conscious beings and certainly not masters of a subservient planet. Our misguided sense of specialness is painfully transformative, and it must be a measure of our stupidity and arrogance that it is taking a global life-threatening crisis to create emergency self-reflection and meaningful dialogue.

The nature of specialness needs to be re-evaluated and released from the egoic narcissism of personal power – as individuals and as a species.

Dr. Richard Tarnas said this in November 2020:

> *"I'm convinced that the entire universe is ensouled and it is a relatively recent superstition on the part of the modern mind to think that we human beings are the only ones to be ensouled. We are expressions of the cosmos and of the earth. We grew out of their life systems and our consciousness is in a very fundamental way, the cosmos's consciousness in human form. But, it's not only in us... it's in all things. Everything is breathing together."*

He goes on to say that we must cease to objectify the world and endure a humbling process of dethronement which is an example of the death-rebirth process involving the crisis of meaning and sense of collapse described above. This is necessary for access to and awareness of a foundational depth that transcends any egocentric notions of superiority and removes that level of self-importance to reveal the true nature of specialness as being an expression of the universe itself, the whole divine cosmological intelligence which lives in and through us all.

Near Death Experiences

Near death experience is always assumed to be what happens when the body is perilously close to expiring. There are many examples of this, and they often describe a remarkably similar experience. It frequently involves an out-of-body perception of what is happening (an operation, a car accident, a hospital bed) and a transition into a tunnel of bright light that draws one forward with a benign and loving energy that is delightful and welcoming – a sense of returning home. It has been repeatedly reported that at the point of the 'tunnel of light' an about-turn occurred and then a return to the body. It was as if 'it was not my time'. There is nothing like a NDE to cause a re-evaluation of one's values and priorities; it usually results in a seismic shift in perception of both. NDE can and does occur at a psychological and experiential level with no apparent threat to the body. William Blake and Neville Goddard (and others) knew this and identified it in their explanations of dying to one state so as to occupy another of one's choosing.

"There is nothing particularly new about the notion that people can "die" and then tell the tale. There are written descriptions of similar experiences in myths and legends going back well over 2,000 years. The sixteenth-century Dutch painter Hieronymus Bosch painted what certainly looks like a near-death experience: a tunnel with angels and a light at one end." [65]

Dr. Peter Fenwick (the internationally renowned neuropsychiatrist and fellow of the Royal College of Psychiatrists) is Britain's leading clinical authority on near-death experiences. He differentiates NDE from TDE – temporary death experience – which is often undergone by those suffering from cardiac arrest. There are many reports of people apparently leaving their bodies and witnessing their own drama of being kept alive through resuscitation attempts on an operating table. To Fenwick this suggests that the mind is capable of separating itself from the brain and therefore able to travel and connect with other nearby minds. (Nearby here does not mean physical proximity.) For him, this possibility allowed access to explanations of coincidences in events and dreams

---

65 Peter Fenwick, *The Art of Dying* – Bloomsbury, 2008

that are shared by people with no mutual knowledge or any form of prior information. This brings us back to Jung's definition of synchronicity – coincidences with meaning – and that nothing occurs by chance. Personal experience that resonates and is reflected in external independent events simultaneously contain profound meaning and significance.

> *"For most people the near-death experience is one of the most profound they will ever have and is vividly remembered throughout their lives. Even if they have no religious faith in particular, many, perhaps most, return believing that death is not the end. And virtually everyone reports that they have lost their fear of death, value their lives more and feel a renewed sense of purpose."* [66]

Synchronicity vs. Karma

In considering the nature of causality and its effect, it is also necessary to clarify the difference between synchronicity and karma. It is curious that Jung wasn't really interested in karma or the notion of

---

66 Peter and Elizabeth Fenwick, *The Art of Dying, ibid.,*

reincarnation; one could quite imagine that he would be. It might have been an issue of belief and association. Jung famously said that he didn't believe anything because he *knew*. If what he knew embraced the acceptance and awareness of the nature of karma, perhaps it was best avoided because it could (and sometimes does) capitulate to a belief system with which he wanted nothing to do.

Karmic cause can be viewed as highly personal, localised and, rather like a bank account, lacking in mystery. Also, it is frequently misunderstood. Karma is the unconscious conditioning that directs one's life; it is partly personal and partly collective, both genetically and from our social conditioning. Many of our thought patterns are inherited, and when we identify with them and believe that they represent who we are, we incarnate into this sense of self. Incarnation is occurring all the time that this assumption is made, which for many people is constant, and it will not cease until the desire to occupy the world of form dissolves. We observed the power of desire together with assumption in chapter 3.

Of course, it is perfectly possible to happily occupy the world of form and be released from the karmic wheel of repetitive reactions and responses; this is the meaning of 'awakening' or 'enlightenment' that breaks into the karmic cycle which then no longer causes suffering. The true understanding of this lies within us; self-inquiry provides far more answers than philosophical discourse does, because to learn through experience enables us to *know*. We reflect the macrocosm and are inhabited by conscious awareness, the activity of which is the dream we are engaged in. As above, so below, as within, so without. When we identify with thought we have forgotten all this and so incarnate yet again.

Jung often applied the term synchronicity when it wasn't strictly appropriate in that no two events were occurring at the same time but there was an unexplained cause for an event or an experience, nonetheless. The philosopher Bernardo Kastrup explains it in his book *Decoding Jung's Metaphysics:* [67]

"Regularities and counter-factual dependencies are observable physical phenomena, empirically accessible to us... Yet, what we call "causality" is not these physical observables themselves, but

67 2019, John Hunt Publishing

that which underlies and explains them – i.e. that which, from behind the scenes, makes them unfold the way they do. As such, causality is a metaphysical organizing principle underlying, and immanent in, physical nature."

If we consider the butterfly effect, where a micro-event results in a macro-event, we can understand from our own experience that we accept the notion of a cause where there might not be one. What caused the butterfly to flap its wings? Take that question further and we eventually arrive at the fundamental accidents within quantum mechanics that are considered to have led to the infinite variety of the universe. Acausality is almost impossible for us to accept and so we readily assume that there must always be causes even though they are undetectable in their huge complexity. However, this assumption has a power of its own as we saw in chapter 3. The assumption(s) itself can contribute to and influence the apparently acausal event; consciousness interacts with matter all of the time, deliberately (on our part) or otherwise. Many scientists find this highly spurious; others (non-scientists) miraculous, and others still, perfectly ordinary.

"...what Jung is saying is that our physical, waking reality is amenable to symbolic interpretation, just as our dreams are. The external world, too, conveys meaning through symbolic expression, 'as if it were the dream of a greater and more comprehensive consciousness.'" (Kastrup, ibid.)

The simultaneous occurrence of a psychic state with a meaningful external/physical event suggests a principle of organisation beyond causality; a metaphysical orchestration of both psychic and physical experience, separately and together. Synchronicity is dependent on the psyche, but purely physical significant coincidences also occur. From a non-dual perspective this is obvious.

Synchronicity provided the foil for linear mechanistic causality which was quite dualistic in an either/or sense (80+ years ago). However, it is possible that Jung's evasion of karmic causality gave way to his own synthesis between the nature of religion and the significance and power of numbers. His absorption of and insight into alchemy is a clear reflection of the art of science, the religion of the human psyche and the omniscience of conscious awareness. An operative alchemist does know the inseparability of art, science, numerology, nature, consciousness, life, and physical death. Jung stated that the religious experience takes place within the psyche, deep in the unconscious where access to archetypes and their significance exists.

Dreams, visions, and symbols are signposts, and it is probable that we ignore them at our peril; in 2021 the planet is already deeply in peril. The anthropocentric position adopted by the mechanistic view of the world and man's place in it has been largely dismissive of the purpose, value and meaning of symbols and archetypes, dreams, and levels of consciousness other than the sentient self. This might be changing, and it probably is, but this transformation began in the 1960s (in the west) with places such as The Esalen Institute in California which had (and still has) a profound influence on the development of human potential and consciousness awareness. It promoted ecology, alternative medicine, mind-body practices and an assimilation of Eastern philosophies, and it was a key player in the counterculture of the 1960s and '70s. In other words, the advancement and insight as to how we are to transform ourselves personally, socially, and then globally, is painfully and dangerously slow. Sixty years on and we are in a global crisis and in sight of planetary mortality. Personal transformation is constantly available to us; it is 'the power of one' in perennial philosophy and is the means by which effective change spreads. 'In the symbol, the world itself is speaking.' *(Tarnas, ibid.,)*

Deeper Meanings from Synchronicities

Jung equated the psyche with the soul, both on a personal level and a collective one and took the view that we are embedded in a larger shared and unified psyche/soul that is evolving through its own spiritual transformations involving us all. Synchronicities tell us that the materialist/mechanistic view of the world in which only the human being carries meaning and purpose cannot possibly be true. By connecting with archetypal sources, we are able to access and experience a deeper meaning, purpose and value to life. Meaningful coincidences are not mysterious; like miracles, they are ordinary, expected and assumed.

> Synchronicities only feel unlikely until we connect with archetypal sources and find the deeper meaning in a world connected in one consciousness.

Richard Tarnas tells a beautiful story illustrating this. He relates it from the words written by Freya Matthews, the Australian eco-philosopher, and that's what the following is also. It is taken from his talk delivered at the Synchronicity Symposium in 2014.

> "'The protagonist in this story was a vine which once grew in my back yard. It was a plant of extraordinary vitality and a Henri Rousseaux-esque aspect with over-sized glossy leaves. I had planted it myself and had had to save it several times, relocating it to more suitable sites in the garden. Eventually, I found a place for it against the side fence where it flourished most exuberantly. I felt a keen affection for it, an involvement with that plant; I watched it grow from day to day and got to know its habit well. Its unreserved joy of life was infectious and it added a lift to my step as I went out each day. It grew happily in the spot that I had chosen for it and after some years it covered the whole fence. One day, however, our neighbour, who detested jubilant foliage of any kind, announced his plan to lay a concrete trench on his side of the boundary. This entailed cutting through the core of the vine's route system and hence certain

and immediate death for the plant. There was nothing I could do; I mourned for my plant-friend. I sat by it, spent time with it. The morning of the execution, I went out onto the veranda to say my last farewells, only to find that the vine had put forth a single extraordinary bloom, a huge yellow trumpet flower. It had never bloomed before and I had no idea that solandras bloomed at all, they being quite rare in gardens so far south. But there it was, a magnificent swan-song in flower. I was profoundly moved, and though the plant was indeed killed that day, I felt that it had given something of itself to me, something precious. Few human responses could have moved me more.'"

Panpsychism

This brings us to the contentious subject of panpsychism. This is the idea that varying degrees of consciousness exist in sub-atomic particles and it is an idea adopted by some of those holding the materialist worldview to offer an explanation of human consciousness. Standard materialism is of the opinion that all matter is unconscious which includes the entire universe including the human brain. This gives rise to 'the hard problem of consciousness' (a phrase coined by Prof. David Chalmers in *The Conscious Mind* (OUP 1996) for physicists and neuroscientists, and some of them concede that an element of consciousness must exist in electrons, protons and atoms from which human consciousness gradually emerges. These are the panpsychists. The word means 'mind everywhere' and begs the question 'how much mind?' And who is able to measure and quantify it?

In his book *Galileo's Error: Foundations for a New Science of Consciousness* (Rider 2019), neuroscientist Philip Goff advocates materialist panpsychism and describes consciousness as being '*located* in the intrinsic nature of the physical world' (my italics). Looking at it from the materialist/reductionist viewpoint, consciousness ascends from the sub-atomic level and increases as it does so. Presumably they think that it reaches its zenith in the human brain. Then there are those who think that the entire cosmos is conscious and that the single organisational system resulting from the big bang emerged into a multitude of forms all sharing the one mind. From this viewpoint consciousness descends from a realm which lies beyond the human mind and the physical world contains different levels of it. Then there is the possibility that the ascent and descent happen simultaneously, and some panpsychists adopt an explanation which is, essentially, materialism with a concession to varying amounts of consciousness in matter. This could be viewed as a form of animism which considers the entire universe to be a living organism, which means that the whole of the natural world is alive with some level of awareness.

Panpsychism finds consciousness in every single thing in the universe. The reverse is also possible: that every single thing in the universe is an attribute of one consciousness.

All of these viewpoints presuppose that things – people, animals, plants, atoms, etc. – *possess* consciousness, that the human brain contains it and that it might be found *in* plants, rocks, animals and particles. There is, however, another view which upends this perception and suggests that only consciousness is conscious and that everything lies within it as a finite, localised focal point. The single, unchanging, infinite reality from which everyone and everything derives their apparently independent existence is consciousness.

The universe is the activity of consciousness. This non-dualism is a reversal of panpsychism in that awareness is not an attribute of anything, but everything is an attribute of it.

'Rupert Squared'

In the Spring of 2020 Rupert Sheldrake and Rupert Spira engaged in a dialogue on the nature of consciousness. We have already met Rupert Sheldrake in earlier chapters; he is a biologist and author best known for his work on morphic resonance. He has since written several books on the convergence of science and spirituality and is both a practising Christian and an advocate of the sun possessing consciousness. It was he who coined the term 'Rupert squared'.

Rupert Spira is an international teacher of the Advaita Vedanta direct path method. He studied with Francis Lucille in India for many years and has written books on the subjects of conscious awareness and the nature of experience. On the face of it, these two philosophers hold opposing views. They certainly come from very different backgrounds – one a scientist, the other not only a life-long philosopher but also a recognised ceramic artist. That they explored their respective ideas with each other was a source of enormous interest, and the fact that they are both English, highly educated, extremely polite and mostly 'enlightened' meant that they afforded each other plenty of space to express their respective ideas and looked for shared perspectives rather than defending their possible differences. I will now outline the core tenets of their conversation.

Rupert Spira's view is that there is a single reality the nature of which is consciousness, and that what we perceive as the physical universe is what the *activity* of consciousness looks like from a localised perspective (a human being). This means that the universe is not an entity made out of matter; it may appear to be made out of matter, but only to a localised mind within that world. He insists that the world is real, but not in the way that we think it is because its reality lies in consciousness and not in matter. This enables the world to be both illusory *and* real. This is a reversal of the accepted notion that the 'dead matter' of the apparent world *gives rise* to consciousness. It is reminiscent of Aldous Huxley in *The Doors of Perception:*

"To make biological survival possible, Mind at Large (consciousness) has to be funnelled through the reducing valve of the brain and nervous system. What comes out at the other end is a measly trickle of the kind of consciousness which will help us to stay alive on the surface of this particular planet." (My brackets).

Rupert Sheldrake approaches this subject from the point of view of the Christian Trinity which he describes as a model of the way in which God interfaces with the world. He describes the Godhead as being beyond the trinity and prior to any possible concept of differentiation. Essentially, this is the connection point between the two Ruperts. Nothing can be apart from Ultimate Being which is all that is. There is nothing else in Ultimate Being (God, conscious awareness, Mind at Large) other than itself from which all things are made. They also shared the perception of I AM THAT, I AM and Sheldrake's years in India with Father Bede and his knowledge of Indian philosophy created an unusual connection that crossed some potential boundaries between them. Their shared experience of the awareness of I AM was revelatory in the sense that the same language had meaning for both and that the ISNESS of things and the AMNESS of human beings vary only by degree. Thoughts, perceptions, and feelings blur the self-awareness of consciousness because these experiences are not conscious in themselves. They arise out of or from consciousness, but are not independently conscious.

When we engage in certain spiritual practices, we are trying to allow consciousness to divest itself of the ephemera of life-situations and experiences to dwell fully in a state of self-awareness. The recognition that can arise from these activities is the work of consciousness unclothing itself of name and form. The multiplicity and diversity of objects and selves losing their capacity to obscure our shared being was also shared by the two Ruperts, and they concluded in a level of mutual agreement.

Death and Dying

It would be interesting to witness a dialogue between them on the subjects of death and dying. It is likely that they might also come to a mutual understanding despite their seemingly different backgrounds and viewpoints. Despite being a Christian, Sheldrake is very open-minded about the possible experiences available once the body has expired. His personal view seems to be that just as we dream during sleep so we will continue to dream after physical death because departure from the body is not new for the mind and has been a regular occurrence for as many years as we have lived. This is because the mind is not the brain which is a physical finite organ and will have died along with the rest of the body.

As we have identified previously, the mind, or Mind, is beyond the body and is a shared phenomenon. This needs some qualification, because the word 'mind' is so commonly used and yet it contains layers of potential meaning. The localised, finite mind that is usually referred to in every day parlance is that which consists of feelings, perceptions, and thoughts. When we say 'I've changed my mind' about some event, what we really mean is that our thoughts and subsequent decisions have altered. This mostly arises from a view of the external world to which this level of mind has limited itself by default. However, all experience is mediated by the one Mind which has no limitations, and its actual nature is conscious awareness which enables us to know the external world through the senses and the internal world through imagination, feeling and emotion. Huxley again:

"Systematic reasoning is something we could not, as a species or as individuals, possibly do without. But neither, if we are to remain sane, can we possibly do without direct perception, the more unsystematic the better, of the inner and outer worlds into which we have been born. This given reality is an infinite which passes all understanding and yet admits of being directly and in some sort totally apprehended. It is a transcendence belonging to another order other than human, and yet it may be present to us as a felt immanence, an experienced participation."

And as he continues, we are reminded of Ernest Becker in chapter 1 and the issue of 'creatureliness':

"To be enlightened is to be aware, always. Of total reality in its immanent otherness – to be aware of it and yet to remain in a condition to survive as an animal, to think and feel as a human being, to resort whenever expedient to systematic reasoning."

Sheldrake also considers the possibility that post-death experience might fulfil beliefs and expectations, so that if you anticipate purgatory you will experience purgatory, or if it is floating on a cloud to a choir of angels, that is what will seem to be happening. His Christianity certainly doesn't presume an anthropomorphised God admitting or refusing entry into a celestial realm.

Spira says that when the so-called body disappears, its reality doesn't, and that experience must be the test of reality. To believe that the world is made out of matter is an illusion; the reality of experience is consciousness, and the disintegration of the body has no impact upon it. Does this mean that experience continues after physical death? He suggests that it might well do in the unravelling of tightly localised consciousness as it gradually rejoins the flow of infinite consciousness. He likens it to a whirlpool in a river as its energy disperses into the flow of the river from which it arose. The process is gradual rather than sudden and immediate. As identified in chapter 2, this is what is known as the *bardos* in Buddhism – a stage of transition or, rather, stages of transition of which there are three: before, during and after; *KU CHU KE; becoming, being, dissolving.*

The Final Sleep

Like Sheldrake, Spira uses the analogy of sleep to assist in an understanding of death, and this involves a challenge to the concept of time. Based on experience (which the Vedantic non-duality teaching is), we know nothing of time when in deep sleep owing to the absence of thought. Linear time is created and needed by thought as a concept to contain events. Without thought this concept collapses and vanishes. Awareness, however, never goes anywhere – there is 'nowhere' for it to go. The fear of death is an egoic response to the belief that objects, events, perceptions and relationships define us, and yet we are perfectly happy to fall asleep each night and often feel huge relief at the prospect of being free from it all. The 'distance' between birth and death is the same as between waking and sleeping – there isn't any. Thought cannot conceive this idea and it is futile to try to; we must be informed by experience, and we do not experience time when asleep. In fact, we don't experience time at all, we only experience now. We think we experience time because the concept of it arose from thought which, as we observed, needs it to function. In his book *Being Aware of Being Aware* (Sahaja Publications, 2017) Rupert Spira writes:

"When the body appears or is born, awareness is not born; when the body ages, awareness does not age; and when the body disappears or dies, awareness does not die or disappear. It remains in the same ageless condition throughout... The finite mind imagines that awareness disappears in deep sleep, but in awareness's experience it is the finite mind that disappears in deep sleep, leaving awareness all alone. Deep sleep is not the absence of awareness; it is the awareness of absence."

Rupert Spira spent more than twenty years studying the Advaita Vedantic tradition and the Tantric tradition of Kashmir Shaivism, which between them cover the direct path inwards and outwards respectively. The Vedantic self-inquiry approach is inward facing and known as the path of discrimination which leads directly to the essential nature of oneself and temporarily (perhaps) turns away from the world of matter to investigate the reality of conscious awareness within. The Tantric path faces outwards and brings the truth arising from Vedanta into the world of the senses, relationships, and objects. Both are intrinsically joined (yogic) in terms of the conscious unveiling of one's experiences, reactions, and behaviour – the way that we perform in the world.

For many people it is the Tantric or outward-looking path that might feel most relevant because it is the world of inclusion and activity.

The Tantric Path

The Tantric concept is described by Ajit Mookerjee in *Kundalini – The Arousal of Inner Energy* (Thames and Hudson, 1982):

> *"Liberation while living is considered in Indian life to be the highest experience – a fusion of the individual with universal. The individual manifestation is like a spark of the cosmos, as the human organism, the microcosm, parallels everything in the macrocosm. The complete drama of the universe is repeated here, in this very body. The whole body with its biological and psychological processes becomes an instrument through which the cosmic power reveals itself. According to Tantric principles, all that exists in the universe must also exist in the individual body. If we can analyse one human being, we shall be able to analyse the entire universe, because it is believed that all is built on the same plane."*

Being the outward path into the world of the senses, responses and consequent experience, the Tantric approach welcomes death as much as life because it is neither resisted nor feared. Its inevitability is assumed and accepted in neutral awareness. The Vedantic inquiry and discernment equips the mind to relinquish the agitation caused by the denial and avoidance of death's inevitability and enables it to enter the outer world with the experiential insight afforded by conscious awareness. Egoic death is to be encouraged; physical death is incidental; the death of conscious awareness is meaningless.

The Jungian anima and animus translate as *dakini* and *daka* in tantra,[68] and their union within each individual is a powerful channel for transcendence of sexual duality while also affording an inner experience of eroticism that is free from projection and dependency. Anima/animus, *dakini/daka* are potent forces within each individual and need to be carefully integrated if we want to avoid being influenced by their often wild and wilful ways, examples of which are evident everywhere, within and without. They personify the male and female attributes of both men and women, an

---

68 Shiva/Shakti in Hindu mythology.

awareness of which is often lacking. The tantric path is to awaken the union of *dakini and daka* within both genders. This is not physical hermaphroditism, but inner psychic androgyny which is the integration of the male and female principles *within oneself;* the outward expression and representation of it is secondary. The term Hermaphrodite in Greek mythology (which is where it holds relevance for human experience), arises from the marriage of Hermes and Aphrodite, whose son became non-binary at the age of fifteen after encountering a water nymph with whom he became physically fused. As with all myths and archetypes, the value of them lies in the internal awareness and awakening that they afford.[69] & [70]

The sexual component of the tantric path is frequently misunderstood, particularly in the west. The ultimate goal is to transcend the duality of male and female so as to become one with universal consciousness; the

---

69 The biological meaning of hermaphroditism regarding dual reproductive organs in some organisms is not appropriate here, but for further reading refer to the exhaustive study by John C. Avise - *Hermaphroditism: A Primer on the Biology, Ecology, and Evolution of Dual Sexuality* - Columbia University Press, 2011.

70 See also Appendix 1 - The Gospel of Thomas – for Christ's sayings regarding gender unification.

potentially transformative power of sexual activity is simply one form of energy that can be used to achieve this. It is a means to a unified end and not the actual goal – it assists in the removal of obstacles that obscure what has always been present. The tantric path provides human beings with a way of being in the mundane world while maintaining the awareness of *being* in the transcendent one. Sexuality in tantra is considered to be sacred and is the essence of the tantric perspective and approach to being in the world; it is the outward path in the world of form, the bridge between the transcendent and the mundane. The intense feeling of 'being in love' to which we attribute the ordeal of *falling* arises from the experience of union, of being 'one with', and it *can* feel inviolate and sacrosanct. The bi-unity of the female and male principles *is* human consummation, and the two becoming one creates the trinity that is to be found in so many religious and spiritual practices. Yogic asanas (yoga meaning to join, to unite) discipline the mind and body, thereby permitting the powerful force of that energy to flow through the physio-psychic plane. A new unity arises and the former two are subsumed within it. Sexuality and spirituality fuse into one energy source known as hierogamy, a derivative of the *Hieros Gamos* – the sacred union, or the divine union of opposites: male/

female; matter/mind; physical/psychic. It is seen as the quintessence of the divine mysteries studied in Greek and Indian cultures, and in the branch of Hinduism known as *Shaivism,* the god Shiva contains the masculine energy and the goddess Shakti the feminine, both of which are divine and alive in both men and women. Shiva is absolute consciousness, the source of everything, the constant awareness of all that is. The qualities of presence, knowing and perfect being are contained within Shiva and are accessible to us through our own awareness and invocation. This is our inner masculine principle. In contrast to the formless energy of Shiva, Shakti is the powerful feminine force of the manifested world which is all pure potential and possibility. It enlivens the subtle body and, in contrast to the repose and stillness of Shiva, Shakti moves and dances when called upon, and can transform the nature of our perception and experience. The union of Shiva and Shakti is the androgyny within us all.[71]

The tantric path is one that awakens the union of male and female within the psyche of both genders. Jung

---

71 For in-depth exploration of Shakti – *Passionate Enlightenment: Women in Tantric Buddhism* by Miranda Shaw. Princeton University Press, 1994.

knew that these tantric traditions were embedded within alchemy, and that they can be found there in their westernised, codified forms. He knew that the unconscious is an essential component of an alchemical process in which we can all participate.

Alchemy

The transformation of the mundane into the transcendent can occur at all levels of existence and Being. It includes the physical, the spiritual and the psychic worlds which form the *Unus Mundus.* This can be represented mythologically as the sacred marriage, or *Hieros Gamos* mentioned above – the alchemical, mythical and yogic representation of the unity of the world. This 'group soul' or 'one soul' is that which animates the entire universe (according to Jung), and its spirit exists in everything – physical, psychic, spiritual, metaphysical. It is called the *anthropos,* the essential nature of which lies within the core of all religions. It can be translated as Christ consciousness, or the Christic principle; in Hindu it is the Atman and Krishna consciousness, and in Buddhism the Buddha-nature, and so on. To experience the *anthropos* is to be aware of the absolute nature of the *Unus Mundus.* Alchemy embraces the darkness (the shadow) as well as the light so that nothing is concealed and hidden from view. It treats the world of mind and matter as one divine union of opposites.

Essentially, all philosophies, mythologies and religions tell the same story; there is only one story which is wrapped up and delivered in a variety of guises. Alchemy is the relationship between consciousness and matter and, while it is none of the above, its principles translate onto all of them. This suggests that they are all expounding the relationship between consciousness and matter in one way or another, an understanding which is rarely acknowledged overtly. It is worth repeating the quote from Chapter 2 by Samael Aun Weor:

> *"Indeed, only one unique and cosmic religion truly exists. This religion assumes different forms according to the times and the needs of humanity. Therefore, religious conflicts are an absurdity, because at their base all religions are only modifications of the universal cosmic religion."* (Ibid.,)

Alchemy does not require any form of belief system because it is based entirely on experiential evidence, both within and without, above and below, consciousness and matter. If there is only one story, in essence, how can there be such a diversity of paths, religions and philosophies trying to express it? Nearly, if not all, established religious practices are founded on ancient guidance, insight, and instruction from different cultures around the world. Each have their own references, parables and languages that were appropriate thousands of years ago in their various cultural environments, but those analogies and metaphors cease to resonate with the same relevance in our evolving experience of the world. [72]

Religion

The language and imagery of Christianity can be counter-productive to an understanding of the oneness of a shared and all-knowing awareness or the fundamental nature of ever-present peace and happiness. On the contrary, the misunderstanding of biblical scripture has caused untold damage on personal and global levels. *A Course in Miracles* is a contemporary application of Christian principles

---

72 For more detailed investigation into alchemy, refer to *Sorcerer's Stone* by Dennis William Hauch – Crucible Books, 2013.

which confirms the biblical message of our true identity, and aims at correcting perception of the world and of ourselves – within and without. This is so that we can learn to alleviate suffering by removing the obstacles to our true nature which is one of love, peace, and happiness. "A Course in Miracles is not about performing miracles in the physical, spectacular sense. The miracles that the Course teaches are the shifts in perception that enable us to view the world through the eyes of love rather than through the eyes of fear." (*From the introduction.)*

The fact that *A Course in Miracles* perpetuates the sense of the individual as a self, with capital letters for god and its pronoun, and adopts masculine referencing throughout, can be an obstacle to accepting its message. It is a dictation from Jesus to Dr. Helen Shucmann, which presumably explains some of this, but doesn't endear it to anyone who may have rejected Christianity partly for those reasons. Words such as atonement, salvation and redemption imply a sense of guilt and unworthiness – the original sin with which Catholics are born – and can inevitably create resistance. Ultimately its teaching is of oneness, beingness, non-duality and the condition of love that is always present and shared by all. Much of the language is certainly beautiful and often poetic which can be a joy to read and dwell on, but the path is long and inevitably Christian, even though its essential teaching goes beyond Christianity.

Buddhism bypasses the inherent guilt of Christianity and goes directly to the immediate availability and awareness of the Buddha nature in all beings, irrespective of their performance-self which might be clouded in distress and suffering. The 'Buddha nature' is a label given by Buddhists to conscious awareness which is free from being anthropomorphised into father, son, and holy ghost.

The language and imagery of Buddhist philosophy is difficult to absorb for many non-Tibetan/Indian/Japanese cultures. The vocabulary can cause a sense of inadequacy and unworthiness and the emphasis on the importance of the master/student or mentor/disciple relationship – so often misunderstood – can perpetuate those feelings and make 'enlightenment' seem remote and difficult. I have quoted Daisaku Ikeda several times already in earlier chapters, but here is an example from *On Attaining Buddhahood in this Lifetime,* (copywrited by the Soka Gakkai in 2011) which could be challenging to assimilate or feel encouraged by:

"A fighting faith through which we take on and overcome the three obstacles and four devils opens the life-state of Buddhahood. There is no attaining enlightenment without struggling against the three powerful enemies. Those who work unceasingly for kosen-rufu are genuine Buddhas... To seek in Buddhism a life of peace and quiet, free of trouble, goes against its basic tenets. The lives of Shakyamuni Buddha and Nicherin Daishonin were fierce struggles, anything but tranquil and trouble-free."

Thirteenth century Japan is hard to relate to; even present-day Japanese culture is remote and exotic by western standards, as are Tibetan and Indian cultures. To grasp the perennial teaching or story, is it necessary to wade through a culturally foreign landscape trying to fathom and absorb metaphors, analogies and imagery that are often difficult and, therefore, laborious and unrelatable? What is the purpose?

Christianity and Buddhism are just two examples of religious philosophy chosen here because I know something of them both, but the inquiry applies to any ancient teaching from which comparatively modern teachings have evolved, but in which they are rooted. There is a tendency to claim Christianity as a western belief system, but of course it isn't, although presumably Jesus spoke to Helen Shucmann in English (with an American accent?)[73] If we divest any religion of its ancient mythologies and cultural traditions which are often obtuse and ripe for misinterpretation, what are we left with? What is the one story? It must be about identity – who and what we truly are, our essential nature of conscious awareness which is always present and which we all share.

We actually know that we operate and perceive at a slightly misguided level because there is a sense of restlessness and longing which sometimes translates into nostalgia, partly because we feel as if we've lost something precious. We temporarily alleviate this restlessness by distracting ourselves in the world of form with the acquisition of objects, people, and substances, and because it's so temporary we have to do it repeatedly; it is never enough. The fact is that you cannot lose something that you are. It is there constantly, in sleep and in death – peace, knowing, love. Everybody longs for this; that's partly why we

---

73 Apparently, Jesus always uses the recipient's vernacular.

look forward to going to sleep because in deep sleep (not the dream state) that's all there is, and of course we are not afraid of it; we love it – it's perfect peace and happiness, the true desire of every human being.

The Value of Rituals

What then, is the purpose of adopting the rituals and behaviours of other cultures from hundreds of years ago? It must be because of the psychological benefits and valued emotions, our principle motivating force. That is the purpose, but not always the reason. The reasons are many and varied and include coercion, guilt, fear, and ignorance, none of which is relevant here. What is relevant is the question as to why anyone with insight into the complex and often distracting packaging of so much spiritual practice continues to engage with rituals and routines which are unnecessary for the achievement of the peaceful open awareness of their true and unassailable nature. Surely, it's because they enjoy the activity of it and therefore receive benefit and value. That's why we choose to do anything.

An analogy might be a journey where the fastest and most efficient route from Manchester to Edinburgh is mostly motorway, but we choose to take a detour via the scenic route on minor roads because of its beautiful countryside which we love. We know that Edinburgh is there; it's always there and we feel secure in the knowledge of that. To go a step further, *we are already in Edinburgh.* Specifically, and with reference to chapter 3, a Buddhist can abide in the understanding of non-duality and live a life informed by the truth of it, and still chant Namu Myo Ho Renge Kyo because it isn't separate from it; it is a part of its expression. The purpose of focusing on the Gohonzon is its reflection of our awareness of our true nature – I AM – which the activity of chanting deepens and strengthens. It can be a meditation in the form of self-investigation, a surrender to the nature of reality through the self-knowledge that is revealed. There can be both a sense of collapse *and* of recognition. This doesn't have to be confined to a twice daily practice or ritual; it gradually becomes an integral aspect of daily activity wherein the meditative nature of Namu Myoho Renge Kyo is always present within as we interact with the world without.

The absolute truth is nameless, formless, and wordless; it is silence. But while in the world of form, relationships, and communication, we adopt the most appropriate and beneficial means to express and share our intentions, feelings, and ideas. This is comparable with the Tantric path of maintaining conscious awareness in the midst of all experience; it is always with you, and although it is easily mislaid in the early stages, gradually distractions cease and all experience becomes imbued with it, effortlessly. It has also been referred to as lucid waking, and meditative chanting facilitates our abidance in the post-egoic state of knowing awareness in any life situation. This sense of abidance, irrespective of our intellectual understanding, may take some time to become truly established, because we have years of conditioning and deeply engrained reactive habits that are not willing to leave without a fight for survival, and are likely to become more petulant and invasive as they realise that they have been discovered for what they really are. It can be likened to experiencing internal tantrums (resistance) and, as with all tantrums at any age, someone needs to be firm and resolute. The effortlessness will eventually follow.

The absolute truth is nameless, formless, and wordless; it is silence.

> *"The principle of 'Least Action' governs everything in physics from the path of a planet to the path of a pulse of light. Least Action is the minimum of energy, multiplied by the minimum of time... Therefore, you must use the minimum of energy and take the shortest possible time... The day you fully realize the power of assumption, you discover that it works in complete conformity with this principle. It works by means of attention, minus effort. Thus, with least action through an assumption you hurry without haste and reach your goal without effort.'* (Neville Goddard, *The Power of Awareness ibid.*,)

The Purpose of Death

Conscious awareness is permanent, the never changing reality of all experience. Indeed, we might say that the purpose of death is to gain an understanding of what death is not and, just as deep sleep releases conscious awareness from its particular location, so it does in death, like a child running joyfully out of school for the summer, free from constraint at last. Lucid waking is another level of lucid dreaming (chapter 3); we are aware of the nature of our experience as belonging to a consciousness beyond our own finite mind – *we are being dreamt.* Our 'night dreams' are not limited to biographical details bizarrely jumbled up to produce non-sensical narratives. Some of it is, certainly, but much of the content has nothing to do with anything we might have experienced, including external input from films, substances, and suggestions. Just as the sub-conscious mind receives information from the conscious mind, it is also receptive to input from the one Mind and knows when this is happening because it is far beyond the experience of the localised, biographical, thought-obsessed mind. That mind could not have imagined it. With this understanding, our current reality becomes more accessible.

It is with considerable relief that we are a part of the activity of the single reality of conscious awareness experiencing itself. And it is up to each of us as to what we do with and about it. This includes nothing at all; simply abide in peaceful contentment. Or take it out into whatever world one may occupy and enjoy the invincibility of true knowing, allowing it to inform all reactions, responses, and activities. Paint pictures, write books, dig gardens – any, and all of it. Or try spreading the word, so to speak, either by simply being, or by talking about these things to others as and when appropriate.

There is a purpose to death which has nothing to do with the body, and there is no need to wait for the body to die to wake up and abide in the peaceful knowing of conscious awareness; it's just that most of us do wait. The purpose of death is to realign with that purposeless purity of being, and if we can carry that awareness into our daily lives and activities, we can become an expression of it. The world of form does evolve in complexity and can have purpose, value and meaning while retaining and resting in the pure being of its source. Consciousness takes the form of perception into which the apparent world appears; it 'falls asleep' to its absolute essence and dreams, which means that it assumes the limitations of the finite mind and brings manifestation into existence. And we do the same, knowingly or not. This creation process is the so-called cognitive big bang which is occurring constantly; it creates the mythical past (memory is myth as is speculation) and the equally mythical future. Just as we wake up from a night dream to find we have been in bed asleep all through the apparent drama, we can, at any time, wake up and realise the actual reality of our experience and the purpose of the dream in which it takes place.

The purpose of death is to realign with that purposeless purity of being.

Leaves of Grass

Oh me! Oh life! of the questions of these recurring,
Of the endless trains of the faithless, of cities fill'd
with the foolish,
Of myself forever reproaching myself, (for who more
foolish than I, and who more faithless?)
Of eyes that vainly crave the light, of the objects
mean, of the struggle ever renew'd,
Of the poor results of all, of the plodding and sordid
crowds I see around me,
Of the empty and useless years of the rest, with the
rest me intertwined,
The question, O me! so sad, recurring—What good
amid these, O me, O life?

Answer.
That you are here—that life exists and identity,
That the powerful play goes on, and you may
contribute a verse.

Walt Whitman

═══════

Coda

Our final performance, and one which is usually steeped in ritual, is the only one from which we are absent (unless we are not). The purpose of planning and arranging a funeral can be its value to those concerned in coming to terms with the event of death, and this sometimes includes the dying person; it can help them to plan their departure, and any performance anxiety is confined to what will have already taken place. They can choose the venue, music, readings, coffin, casket, and reception – and many do, those who have enough forewarning and are not in a state of resistance and denial. Even if they are not personally involved, for whatever reason, those responsible feel strongly that the performance should be 'what they would have wanted'. Within families, this can be contentious. Details aside, the ritual of departure is significant in most cultures, all of which retain particular codes and behavioural expectations. It is a grand performance of display, including one of respect whether it is felt or not. Grief is entirely different.

Most people are familiar with the existence of the Egyptian and Tibetan Books of the Dead, but less aware of the number and variety of Books of the Dead from elsewhere, including western Christianity which is usually referred to as *Ars Morendi (The Art of Dying)*. Literature on the subjects of death and dying was prolific in Europe towards the end of the Middle Ages, probably because death was also. And, unlike today, it was highly visible and therefore a real presence in daily life. Famines, plagues, and epidemics could rapidly wipe out vast numbers of people, and the public execution of heretics, alleged witches and other miscreants was commonplace. It was a long period of intense uncertainty and fear which can be seen in much of the art of that time. The immense power of ritual for the deceased takes many forms across the spectrum of spiritual practices which includes the increasingly popular humanitarian funerals where there is no liturgical framework to adhere to; the nature of the performance is chosen and choreographed by the participants. There are also more extreme and spectacular funereal customs such as the Tibetan Sky Burial where the corpse is prostrated on a mountain for vultures to devour – also known as the 'Bird Scattering'. There is a ritual of blood-letting in the ancient Maya tradition, and more bird symbolism in the Mystery of the Plumed Serpent in the Nahuatl Book of the Dead. The Christian theme of death and resurrection exists in a great many religions worldwide and for some it means the prohibition of cremation. The Catholic Church only allowed cremation from 1963 under the condition that the ashes were not scattered nor kept in a non-sacred place. This is so as not to suggest a disbelief in bodily resurrection. The belief in resurrection is also why orthodox Jews are buried rather than cremated, and this takes place as quickly as possible following the death, after which there are seven days of *shiva* where the body is never left alone and family members and close friends visit the house and sit with it together. The correct performance of ritual in Hinduism can be found in its Vedic scriptures and, although they also believe in a form of reincarnation, their attitude to fire is very different. They consider it to be the conduit of mortality to godliness (Brahman) via the god of fire *Agni*. Nearly all Hindus are cremated. Whatever the script, whoever conducts and directs, and with all forms and levels of audience participation, the funeral is as powerful and purposeful as any ritual during our lifetime.

There is a pithy phrase 'life is not a rehearsal'. In fact, it turned up yet again in an article recently: Joe Moran reviewing Oliver Burkeman's book *Four Thousand Weeks: Time and How to Use It*:

> "*Our problem with time', Burkeman writes, is that we refuse to see that 'this life, with all its flaws and inescapable vulnerabilities, its extreme brevity, and our limited influence over how it unfolds, is the only one we'll get a shot at.' Well, yes: life's not a rehearsal. And we need to live in the present and not mind so much about whether the future will conform to our desires for it. We all know this.*" (The Guardian, 4th September 2021).

Life almost certainly is a rehearsal, once we understand and realise what death is not. To assert that it isn't is to imply that it's in a constant state of performance, with which I obviously agree, but every performance is a rehearsal for the next performance and that is how we live, die, and incarnate constantly. The care and attention that we apply depends on the overriding desire and aspiration at any moment, but however 'long it takes', the dissolution into pure conscious awareness is inevitable. This particular display of creativity is over, that's all.

Probably the reading most frequently offered at funerals is Dylan Thomas's *Do Not Go Gentle Into That Good Night.* This is an exhortation to resist the inevitability of what has already occurred, thereby causing more suffering, and an aggressive oratory of denial and resentment. This is no aspersion on the poem itself nor of Thomas, but it is to question the motive for choosing to read it aloud as if to the deceased. The physical organism no longer functions, and so this ritualistic delivery of a poem about anger and resistance is inappropriate and unhelpful (to mourners). The one for whom they grieve has already gone, gently or not. Whether it's your father or a stranger, there is another and more benign way of navigating and acknowledging the process of dying.

Go gently into that bright light

There is nowhere to go, and more light than you can ever have witnessed. There is no need to burn and rave, only to remain quiet and tranquil.

However wise, darkness is neither right nor not right; it is meaningless.

Goodness is always questionable and that is the only cause for tears.

Hedonism usually wears itself out, and what lies ahead will help in the understanding of the illusory loss.

There was no need to be so seriously serious after all.

And now be, be on the happy peaceful height.

No more tears; light that is yet unimaginable awaits, and a luminous peaceful calm.

APPENDIX 1

The Gospel of Thomas

And he said:

'Whoever finds the meaning of these words will not taste death.'

The Gospel of Thomas is part of the Nag Hammadi library which was discovered in 1945 in an Egyptian cave, probably a tomb. It consists of thirteen manuscripts which contain forty-eight separate works that are described as gnostic, (protonostic by scholars more recently), and the Gospel of Thomas is one of them. Unlike the canonic gospels, there isn't a narrative, but rather a collection of 114 sayings attributed to Jesus. This text has also been called a Book of Wisdom, revealing that salvation is achieved through self-knowledge and the awareness of the power that we all possess to create our own experience. It contains no events – no virgin birth, miracles, crucifixion nor resurrection. It opens with an allusion to twins as if Jesus had a twin brother (Thomas), but this is too literal an interpretation of what is essentially a mystical manuscript. The 'twin' is all of us; we can create just as Jesus did. Gnosis = self-knowledge = divinity = infinite consciousness.

'Let not him who seeks desist until he finds. When he finds he will be troubled; when he is troubled, he will marvel, and he will reign over the universe.'

When we discover that all that we desire lies within our capacity to realise, it is troubling because it contradicts all that we have been taught and come to accept – a conditioning that is hundreds of years old. This challenges our sense of identity as it reveals our misconceptions about it. To feel divested of the labels that have thus far defined us in the world is bound to be troubling, but once this confusion has been overcome, of course we will marvel – it is profoundly life-altering. Understanding that all potential lies within each of us means that we have absolute reign over our lives, within and without, above and below, heaven on earth.

The reason for this and other esoteric texts being 'lost' is that in 325 AD the then Bible was heavily edited under Emperor Constantine's rule. In fact, they were deliberately and carefully hidden in a large six foot tall jar to be discovered at some point in the future. It wasn't Constantine who edited the manuscripts, but his bishops who had at least two agendas: to unify the Holy

Roman Empire under one single universal (Catholic) church, and to remove any suggestion that everyone possesses the same personal authority and power as Jesus. By editing out the mystical truths contained in the forty-eight manuscripts, all strength, influence, and potency remained externalised and wholly appropriated by a governing force that was fearful, threatening and debilitating. With an understanding of personally embodied infinite consciousness, there is no need for churches, authority, or priests; nor for salvation, redemption, and worship, all of which is highly threatening to a government attempting to control a vast empire under a single religious doctrine.

Here is an example of withheld information to illustrate the previous postulation. In Matthew 7:7 the verse reads:

> 'Ask and it will be given unto you; seek and ye shall find; knock and the door will be opened.'

What we need to know is how does it work? We are bound to think that asking is an act of language, of the correct wording, without sounding avaricious and with an understandable justification for whatever it is. It is none of these. The language of manifestation is feeling, not words; it is assumption in the present tense. The unedited version found in The Gospel of Thomas reads:

> *'Ask without hidden motive and be surrounded by your answer. Be enveloped by your desire, that your gladness be full.'*

This is Neville Goddard; it is the Bhagavad Gita, Advaita Vedanta and Buddhism. If you look within yourself deeply enough you will find the divine energy as the source of your being. This interior searching and the transformation of our sense of identity is the essence of The Gospel of Thomas, and is what Jesus said to him.

In verse 77 Jesus said:

> *'It is I who am the light which is above them all. It is I who AM the all. From me did the all come forth, and unto me did the all extend. Split a piece of wood and I AM there. Lift up a stone and you'll find me there.'*

And later in verse 113 after he has been asked when the kingdom will appear he replies:

'It will not come by waiting for it. It will not be a matter of saying "here it is" or "there it is". Rather, the kingdom is spread out upon the earth, and men do not see it.'

This describes the One Consciousness within which all things have their being. It explains the presence and immediacy of whatever the kingdom of heaven means to anyone and the necessary conscious awareness to see it. This is the meaning of 'the light'. Any saying that includes 'I AM' refers to everyone; we are all 'I' and therefore the light of consciousness can be found in a split piece of wood and under a stone.

'Jesus said, "If they ask you, 'Where do you come from?' tell them, 'We've come from the light, the place where light came into being by itself, established itself, and appeared in their image.'"
"If they ask you, 'Is it you?' then say, 'We are its children, and we're chosen by its living Source.'"
"If they ask you, 'What is the sign of your source in you?' then say, 'It is movement and rest.'"

Rest is our inner experience and movement is our outward performance into the world. The truth and the peace that we can abide in within, we can then take out into the world with which we interact without being distracted, without losing sight of the Source. There are those who choose not to make the outward journey into the world of activity and interaction, but to remain in the state of a contemplative life. Cyprian Smith:

'Paradox is present in the process of movement, because all things do flow forth from God and back again, the flowing and returning are continual and simultaneous, so that in a sense everything is always both "outside" and "inside", as in the formula "going out yet remaining within"... Paradox is also present in the metaphysical relationship between God and Creature, because both are in a sense "being" and both are, in another sense, "nothing". What is more, the gulf between Creator and creatures is paradoxical, because it both can, and cannot, be bridged.'

'Make two into One
and the inner as the outer
and the outer as the inner,
the above as the below,
the male and female
into a single One.

So the male isn't male and
the female isn't female anymore.'

'Whoever finds the meanings of these words will not taste death.'

APPENDIX 2

Mundus Imaginalis

Mundus Imaginalis or the Imaginary and the Imaginal is a term coined by the French philosopher and theologian Henry Corbin (14th April 1903 – 7th October 1978). He was also a professor of Islamic philosophy and was instrumental in developing the course and direction that the study of this took from around 1946. One of his principal viewpoints and among the most influential was that the imagination is the source of creation, and that prayer is the supreme act of the creative imagination. He was highly concerned with the potential constraints and hermeneutic pitfalls in translation and often wrote quite extensively on how he arrived at a certain turn of phrase, *mundus imaginalis* being one of them. Even reading his paper on this subject alone, we are going from Persian to French to Latin and finally to English, and all in an attempt to understand the meaning of *NA-KOJA-ABAD* or 'the land of nowhere', 'the eighth climate'. Following are some examples: [74]

---

74 Jung, Buddhism, and the Incarnation of Sophia – translated by Jack Cain. Pub., Inner Traditions, Rochester, Vermont 2019 (English copyright).

'The word Na-koja-abad does not designate something like extended being, in the dimensionless state. The Persian word abad certainly signifies a city, a cultivated and peopled land, thus something extended… thus the name Na-koja-Abad: a place outside of place, a "place" that is not contained in a place, that permits a response, with the gesture of the hand, to the question "where?" But when we say, "To depart from the where," what does that mean?'

'But an odd thing happens: once this transition is accomplished, it turns out that henceforth this reality, previously internal and hidden, is revealed to be enveloping, surrounding, containing what was first of all external and visible, since by means of interiorization, one has departed from that external reality. Henceforth, it is spiritual reality that envelops, surrounds, contains the reality called material. That is why spiritual reality is not "in the where." **It is the "where" that is in it.** Or rather, it is itself the "where" of all things; it is, therefore, not itself in a place, it does not fall under the question "where?"'

'What is that intermediate universe? It is the one we mentioned a little while ago as being called the "eighth climate." For all of our thinkers, in fact, the world of extension perceptible to the senses includes the seven climates of their traditional geography. But there is still another climate, represented by that world which however, possesses extension and dimensions, forms and colours, without their being perceptible to the senses, as they are when they are properties of physical bodies. No, these dimensions, shapes, and colors are the proper object of imaginative perception or the "psycho-spiritual senses"; and that world, fully objective and real, where everything existing in the sensory world has its analogue, but not perceptible by the senses, is the world that is designated as the eighth climate. The term is sufficiently eloquent by itself, since it signifies a climate outside of climates, a place outside of place, outside of "where" (Na-koja-Abad!).'

This is *mundus imaginalis,* a dimension beyond the apparent limitations of most waking human experience. It is the world of the Platonic archetypes of light, of the collective unconscious described, explored and experienced by Jung. It lies beyond the limited perception of the waking mind, but still within consciousness itself, as of course it must. When we refer to 'reality' we usually mean the single perspective of it that we share as human beings, and that we label as 'the world'. But it is only a part of reality, and a small one. Animals see and experience other aspects of it altogether and it is just as 'real'. The vastness of the *mundus imaginalis* is not possible to conceive with the conceptual mind, but we can access it, and do so sometimes when asleep. Another way is through art which, at its finest, draws on this timeless realm of the imaginary and the imaginal and manifests it for others to share in the experience. That is why we are so compelled by the best of it, because it expresses the ineffable and is described *and felt* at times as 'not of this world'. How, for example, could a deaf Beethoven compose the late quartets? They would be supernatural enough even if he could hear, and the truth is that, in the realm he occupied, he *could.* Many artists access the personal unconscious, the dream state and, while the validity of this work might not be in doubt (unless it is), something profound can be absent, that quintessential element for which there are no words, which, conversely, usually results in an excessive amount of discursive analysis. There are times when anyone might experience an awareness of another dimension while awake – and so often dismiss it as illusory – when in fact it's all the other way around; other levels of mind are able to interact in particular circumstances, and often do.

In the pure, unfocused, vibration of consciousness there are no things, people, nor physical world. As the vibration gradually intensifies, imaginal creativity is activated, independent of a physical organism. Henry Corbin:

> '[What is] the organ that permits penetration into the mundus imaginalis, the migration to the "eighth climate"? What is the organ by means of which that migration occurs – the migration that is the return ab extra ab intra (from the exterior to the interior), the topographical inversion (the intussusception)? It is neither the senses nor the faculties of the physical organism, nor is it the pure intellect, but it is that intermediate power whose function appears as the preeminent mediator: the Active Imagination... It is the organ that permits the transmutation of internal spiritual states, into vision-events symbolizing with those internal

states. It is by means of this transmutation that all progression in spiritual space is accomplished, or, rather, this transmutation is itself what spatializes that space, what causes space, proximity, distance and remoteness to be there.'

APPENDIX 3

Philosophia Perennis

The perennial philosophy describes the timeless truth that lies at the heart of all religions, the single divine principle and primordial wisdom that validates and binds them, despite their seemingly conflicting viewpoints. These arose largely because of the rapid development of science and materialism during the Renaissance together with the increased secularisation of society which undermined the traditional cultural exclusivity of religious practices in the west. The ability to travel more easily resulted in greater exposure to other spiritual practices, which led to some crises of conflict when sensing that one's personal and exclusive path to the truth might not be the only one after all. The term *Philosophia Perennis* was coined by Agostino Steuco (1497 – 1548) as neo-platonic philosophy developed with the ideas expounded by Marsilio Ficino and Giovani Pico. The transcendentalists appropriated it in the early nineteenth century, and the Theosophical Society popularised it further towards the century's end.

In 1921 a book by René Guénon was published entitled *Theosophy: History of a Pseudo-Religion*[75] in which he

---

75 Pub., Sophia Perennis, Hillsdale NY, first English edition 2003.

criticises Madame Blavatsky and the Society along with other occult, spiritist and masonic movements at that time. In particular, he denounced what he saw as their misguided interpretations of Eastern philosophy. He had been initiated into Sufism in 1910 and wrote extensively on Eastern metaphysical doctrines throughout his life, one of his aims being to adapt them for Western spiritual sensibilities. In 1927 his seminal book *The Crisis of the Modern World* was published,[76] on the basis of which he is widely regarded as the key founder of the perennial philosophy. In it, he iterates the (then) modern world view as being in denial of the metaphysical and transcendent, and far more profane than sacred in its prioritisation of reason and rationality. He regarded the esotericism of the world's religions to be the unifying principle, and the exotericism to have an agenda promoting separation, division, and potential fundamentalism. As outlined in chapter 3 and in appendix 1, the mysticism of Christianity was severely compromised in order to manage the Roman Empire, thereby exotericising selected doctrine and concealing the rest.

The exposition of Truth through revelation has been renewed through the ages according to the time, place,

---

[76] Pub., ibid., 4th edition with revised translation 2001.

and cultural need, to remind and reinstate the sacred and the transcendent. Its expression through art and artefacts permeates every tradition in the world and is not only appreciated but longed for and needed in all forms of civilisation. Indeed, it largely defines a civilisation. Those regarded as the initiators of current perennial philosophical thought all had a profound connection with and insight into the necessity and power of art. Titus Burckhardt (1908 – 1984) wrote extensively on sacred art, particularly Islamic art, as well as on alchemy and the spiritual symbolism of metalurgy. Martin Lings (1909 – 2005) discusses the paradox between the modern myth of progress and the ancient one of eternal reality in his book *Ancient Beliefs and Modern Superstitions.* He discovered the work of René Guénon while reading English at Oxford and also that of Frithjof Schuon, a metaphysician and Perennialist who wrote widely on sacred art, anthropology and the essential Truth contained within all divine revelations. Lings travelled to Basle to meet Schuon, and became a lifelong disciple of his, which included the adoption of Islam.

The third of what are considered to be the three founders of Perennial Philosophy is Ananda Coomaraswarmy (1877 – 1947), one of whose many missions was to educate the West about Indian art, and in 1917 he became the first Keeper of Indian Art in the Boston Museum of Fine Arts. During his time there he wrote about traditional metaphysics and symbolism and defined himself as a metaphysician of the *Sophia Perennis* or perennial wisdom. Although he was born into the Hindu religion, he did much to reinstate traditional Buddhism and was also immersed in Greek metaphysics and the union of Platonism and Vedanta.

The Perennialist viewpoint is not to be confused with *tolerance* which implies that all religions might contain some aspect of truth and is essentially concessionary. Also, it does not preclude engaging with any of the various expressions of the one Truth underpinning them all. Buddhism is probably the most widely adopted philosophical practice to fulfil this role, perhaps partly because god is not a doctrinal issue. Marco Pallis (1895 – 1989) considered himself to be a pilgrim of Tibetan Buddhism as well as being a Perennialist (and a professional musician). He knew René Guénon, Frithjof Schuon and Ananda Coomaraswarmy and shared their spiritual perspective, but chose Tibetan Buddhism as his personal expression of it. This is possible without any sense of exclusivity or specialness, feeling 'chosen' and thereby self-righteous. On the contrary, adoption of a spiritual practice can form the very bridge that enables the connection that is sought.

> "In fact, everything has been said already, though it is far from being the case that everyone has always understood it. There can be, therefore, no question of presenting new truths. However, what is needed in our time, and indeed in every age as it moves away from the origins of revelation, is to provide some people with keys fashioned afresh; keys no better than the old ones, but merely more elaborated and reflective, in order to help them rediscover the truths written in an eternal script from the very substance of the spirit."[77]

---

77 Frithjohn Schuon – *Esotericism as Principle and as Way* – New translation 2019 World Wisdom Inc.

BIBLIOGRAPHY

Allwright, Pat – *Basics of Buddhism* Taplow Press, 1998

Becker, Ernest – *The Denial of Death*, The Free Press, Simon & Schuster, 1973

Brown, Richard and Gerbarg, Patricia – *The Healing Power of Breath*, Shambala Boulder, 2012

Brule, Dan – *Just Breathe*, Simon & Schuster, 2017

Cheetham, Tom – *Imaginal Love: The Meanings of Imagination in Henry Corbin and James Hillman*, Spring Publications, Inc. Thompson, Conn, 2015

—— *All the World an Icon: Henry Corbin and the Angelic Function of Beings*, North Atlantic Books, Berkley, 2012

Childre, Doc and Howard, Martin – *The Heartmath Solution*, Harper Collins, 1999

Corbin, Henry – *Jung, Buddhism, and the Incarnation of Sophia: Unpublished Writings from the Philosopher of the Soul*, Inner Traditions, 2014

Coujin, Tom – Online forum, 2018

Daffern, Thomas – *Multilingual and Multifaith Dictionary of Peace and Global Philosophy*, IIPSGP Publications, 2009

Daishonin, Nichiren – *Japanese Collected Writings*, Taplow Press, WND, Soka Gakkai, 1999

Dalai Lama – *The Book of Transformation*, Harper Collins, 2000

Ellis, Normandi – *Imagining the World into Existence*, Bear & Co., 2012

English, Charlie – *The Gallery of Miracles and Madness*, William Collins, 2021

Fenwick, Peter and Elizabeth – *The Art of Dying*, Bloomsbury, 2008

Goddard, Neville – *The Essential Neville Goddard*, Merchant Books, 2015

Grof, Stanislav and Christina – *Holotropic Breathwork; Holotropic Mind; Beyond Death*, SUNY Press, 2010

Grof, Stanislav – *The Art of Living and Dying as told in the Ancient Books of The Dead*, Thames and Hudson, 1973

Hare, David – *The Buddha in Me, The Buddha in You*, Rider, Penguin Random House, 2016

Hillman, James – *A Blue Fire; Alchemical Psychology*, Spring Publications, 2015

Hogan, Clare – *The Alchemy of Performance Anxiety: Transformation for Artists*, Free Association Books, 2018

Holecek, Andrew – *Preparing to Die*, Snow Lion, 2013

—— *Dream Yoga*, Sounds True, 2016

Hopkins, Avery – *Alchemical Mercury: mind in matter*, Kymia Arts, 2015

Huxley, Aldous – *The Doors of Perception*, Chatto & Windus, 1954

—— *The Perennial Philosophy*, Harpers Perennial, Reprint Edition, 2009

Ikeda, Daisaku – *A New Humanism*, Weatherhill, 1996

—— *Unlocking the Mysteries of Birth and Death*, SGI, 2021

—— *On Attaining Buddhahood in This Lifetime*, World Tribune Press, 2011

Jacobs, Alan – *The Gnostic Gospels*, Watkins, 2006

Kastrup, Bernardo – *More than Allegory*, Iff Books, 2016

—— *Brief Peeks Beyond*, Iff Books, 2015

—— *Science Ideated*, Iff Books, 2021

—— *Decoding Jung's Metaphysics*, Iff Books, 2021

Kolk, Bessel van der – *The Body Keeps the Score*, Penguin Random House UK, 2014

Kubler-Ross, Elisabeth – *On Death and Dying*, Tavistock/Routledge, 1970

—— *On Life After Death*, Celestial Arts, Berkley, California, 1991

Lucille, Francis – *The Perfume of Silence*, Truespeech Publications, 2006

Mate, Gabor – *When the Body Says No.* Vermillion, Penguin Random House, 2019

Mattison, Mark – *The Gospel of Thomas*, Createspace Independent Publishing Platform, 2015

McCraty, Rollin – *The Coherent Heart: Heart-Brain Interactions, Psychophysiological Coherence, and the Emergence of System-Wide Order*, Institute of Heartmath, 2006

McGilchrist, Iain – *The Master and His Emissary*, Yale University Press, 2019 edition.

—— *The Matter with Things*, Perspectiva Press, 2021

McKeown, Patrick – *The Oxygen Advantage*, Piatkus, 2015

Mookerjee, Ajit – *Kundalini – The Arousal of Inner Energy*, Thames and Hudson, 1982

Moore, Thomas – *Ageless Soul*, Simon & Schuster, 2017

Nestor, James – *Breath – The Science of a Lost Art*, Penguin Random House UK, 2020

Porges, Stephen – *The Polyvagal Theory: Neurophysiological Foundations of Emotions, Attachment, Communication, and Self-Regulation*, W.W.Norton & Co., 2017

Preece, Rob – *The Alchemical Buddha: Introducing the Psychology of Buddhist Tantra*, Mudra Publications, 2000

Purce, Jill – *The Mystic Spiral: Journey of the Soul*, Thames & Hudson, 1974

Rilke, Maria Raine – *Letters to a Young Poet*, NY Penguin Books, 2013

Rinpoche Sogyal – *The Tibetan Book of Living and Dying*, Rider, Random House, 1992

Samuels, Julia – *This Too Shall Pass*, Penguin Life, PRH, 2017

Sheldrake, Rupert – *Science and Spiritual Practices*, Coronet (Hodder & Staunton), 2018

—— *The Science Delusion*, Hodder & Stoughton, 2012

—— *Ways To Go Beyond and Why They Work: Seven Spiritual Practices in a Scientific Age*, Coronet, Hodder & Stoughton, 2019

Smith, Cyprian – *The Way of Paradox*, Darton, Longman & Todd, 1987, 2004

Spira, Rupert – *Being Aware of Being Aware*, Sahaja Publications, 2017

—— *The Transparency of Things*, Sahaja Publications, 2016

Tarnas, Richard – *Cosmos and Psyche: Imitations of a New World View*, Viking Penguin, 2006

—— *The Passion of the Western Mind*, Ballantine Books (a division of Random House, Inc.), New York, 1991

Tolle, Eckhart – *A New Earth*, Penguin Books, 2005

Wallace, B. Alan – *Embracing Mind, The Common Ground of Science and Spirituality*, Shambala Publications Inc., 2008

Weor, Samael Auon – *The Perfect Matrimony*, (originally published in Spanish 1950), Glorian Publishing, 2010

Zimmerman, Jens – *Hermeneutics*, Oxford University Press, 2015